LONDON BOROUGH OF BARNET

D0480335

HAPPINESS,
A Mystery

ALSO BY SOPHIE HANNAH

Culver Valley Series Crime Novels

Little Face
Hurting Distance
The Point of Rescue
The Other Half Lives
A Room Swept White
Lasting Damage
Kind of Cruel
The Carrier
The Telling Error
The Narrow Bed

Standalone Crime/Mystery Novels

The Orphan Choir
A Game For All The Family
Did You See Melody?
Haven't They Grown
The Understudy (with Holly Brown, Clare Mackintosh and B. A. Paris)

Hercule Poirot Mysteries

The Monogram Murders
Closed Casket
The Mystery of Three Quarters
The Killings at Kingfisher Hill

Self-Help Books

From Resentment to Contentment – How to hold a Grudge:
The Power of Grudges to Transform Your Life

HAPPINESS,
A Mystery

& 66 attempts to solve it

Sophie Hannah

PROFILE BOOKS

First published in Great Britain in 2020 by
PROFILE BOOKS LTD
29 Cloth Fair
London ECIA 7JQ
www.profilebooks.com

Published in association with Wellcome Collection

183 Euston Road, London NWI 2BE

Wellcome Collection publishes extraordinary books that explore
health, science, life, art and what it means to be human.

Happiness, A Mystery accompanies the season 'On Happiness'
at Wellcome Collection, 27 May – 11 October 2020.

Copyright © Sophie Hannah, 2020

1 3 5 7 9 10 8 6 4 2

Typeset in Caslon by James Alexander at Jade Design
Printed and bound in Great Britain by
Clays Ltd, Elcograf S.p.A.

The moral right of the author has been asserted.

All rights reserved. Without limiting the rights under copyright
reserved above, no part of this publication may be reproduced,
stored or introduced into a retrieval system, or transmitted, in
any form or by any means (electronic, mechanical, photocopying,
recording or otherwise), without the prior written permission of
both the copyright owner and the publisher of this book.

A CIP catalogue record for this book is available from the British Library.

ISBN 978 1 78816 294 4
eISBN 978 1 78283 575 2

For all my Dream Authors,
who have been a joy and an inspiration

Contents

Introduction

Why 66?

I assume you know what I'm talking about. Right? I'll give you a minute to work it out.

Welcome back. Hopefully, you just looked again at this book's cover and noticed that the title contains the word 'mystery' and the subtitle is 'and 66 attempts to solve it'. Yet in the Contents list, there's a chapter called 'The 65 Days'. And 65 is the number that comes before 66. Is this pure coincidence, or is there a mystery to be solved?

Here is my recommendation: wherever possible, treat anything you can as a mystery. Why? Because mysteries make life better. I love mysteries, including the desperately-craving-an-answer part, more than I love their solutions. Definite answers shut down possibilities, while an unsolved puzzle ignites our imagination and invites us to think, 'What if it turns out to be something shocking and unguessable that will well and truly blow my mind?' Then we start to imagine how exhilarated we'll feel when we encounter that unimaginable, mind-blowing solution.

I love mysteries so much that I have a tendency to invent them where they don't exist. I've done this since childhood. Age seven, on a family holiday in Lytham St Annes, I saw two cars driving along a road, one behind the other. 'I wonder why that second car is chasing the first one,' I said to my parents.

They explained that there was no mystery; the two cars had nothing to do with each other. I refused to accept this hypothesis. I wanted and needed a better story.

I'm not going to dwell on The Two-Cars Mystery, because I never solved it and never will – not unless I go to Lytham St Annes to investigate, and I refuse on principle ever to go there again. (It was supposed to be a seaside holiday, and guess what? The sea was not there – like, *at all* – for the whole time that we were. Where was it? I don't know: another mystery. There was a beach, and there were slightly damp mudflats stretching as far as the eye could see, but there was no sea for me to swim in. I was too young to understand about tides, and I'm glad I didn't. I wouldn't have approved.)

If solved and never-to-be-solved mysteries are equally disappointing, it's clear what the ideal is: a puzzle that makes you want to hunt for its solution, happy in the knowledge that there's a fair chance of success.

I'm delighted to be able to present you with that very thing. I'd like to invite you to be my sidekick as I investigate the mystery of happiness. I should probably say 'mysteries', plural. What is happiness? How does one pursue and/or achieve it? Where is it to be found, and with whom?

If you noticed the 65/66 discrepancy before I drew it to your attention, well done. You are perfect sidekick material. If you didn't, do not be disheartened – there's another significant clue in this introduction and you might notice that instead. If you haven't already, don't give up. (NB: There is no limit to how often you can read a book's introduction before proceeding to Chapter 1.)

Let's do a feasibility study before we start our investigation. Is the puzzle of happiness definitely solvable? Isn't it, rather, something that people have opinions about, with no right answer? Well, if happiness is real, then it must be possible to define it and to suggest ways to increase our chances of achieving it if we want to.

All right, you might say, but that's equally true of love or any other human experience. Or pies. Some people think a pie must have pastry covering its entire surface area in order to qualify for the description, while others believe that a stew in a dish with a pastry topping can legitimately be called a pie. (Those crazy fools! I bet they're the same people who book seaside holidays without any sea.) So, why not investigate pies, or the meaning of love? Why happiness?

I was drawn to this specific mystery by my own personal happiness-related dilemma. That's also what led me to have my first ever one-to-one session with a life coach, and I'm going to invite you to be a fly on the wall at that session in a moment, so that you can experience the beginning of the mystery in the most authentic way possible. After all, as any fan of the detective fiction genre knows, the main detective, the sidekick and the reader must all have equal access to the clues at all times. In this case, you're the sidekick *and* the reader, and I don't want to hear any complaints about that being too much work, okay?

Good. I'm glad we agree. Let's proceed to my first (but by no means last) session with a life coach, which contained a revelation so startling that it called into question my whole belief system about how the world works.

1

A Session with a Life Coach

Her name is Katherine. I find her online, and see that she offers life coaching via Skype, which is brilliant and convenient, because she lives in America, and I live in Cambridge, England. I could have found an English life coach and met her in person, and indeed this is what I've always done in the past with psychotherapists, but for life coaching I wanted a bona fide American. Life coaching sounds so much like an American invention that I wasn't even willing to Google it to check that I was right. Just as seafood is often dodgy in restaurants that are too far from the coast, I decided that American life coaching – coming straight from the source – had to be the best kind.

Katherine also has the advantage of looking exactly like my idea of an American life coach: bouncy hair, glossy make-up, good skin, a persuasive smile full of well-proportioned white teeth. Not only does she look perfect for my purposes, her office does too: white walls, cream blinds at the windows, light wood floors. On a white-painted table, a potted plant and a framed photograph are positioned far enough apart to suggest that one or both might be claustrophobic.

This is great. A life coach's walls should be white and uncluttered, and any space inhabited by a life coach should be mainly empty. I firmly believe in the innate superiority of minimalism. My house in Cambridge is full of messy piles of stuff that I'm too busy to sort out and my every wall is covered from top to bottom with badly hung, brightly coloured paintings that probably clash with one another – but that's fine for me, because I'm a flawed human in search of help. Also, I love looking forward to the big decluttering and sprucing up of my house that I keep promising myself as a future treat, when I finally have the time.

Framed and hanging above the table in Katherine's office, between the photograph and the plant, there's an inspirational quote: 'The pain you feel today is the strength you feel tomorrow.' I agree with the sentiment, and I'm pleased that Katherine has it on display. It's precisely what I'd hope to find in the immediate vicinity of an American life coach. Fleetingly, I think of a house I once visited in suburban England that had motivational slogans stencilled on many of its walls. It also had, above the bath, a large tile with 'Bathe' painted on it and one saying 'Sit' directly above the loo. I remember thinking that I didn't want to be helped with my motivation by anyone who could fail to realise why putting the word 'Sit' above a toilet wasn't the best idea. Katherine would never have made that mistake.

'Let's begin,' she says. 'What do you need help with?'

It's ten o'clock at night in England; earlier in America. I'm nervous about the conversation we're going to have, in a way that I've never been when I've spoken to English psychotherapists face to face. Talking to an American life coach on Skype feels a little bit … not exactly sinful, but almost like a secret treat – like waiting until everyone's gone to bed and then scoffing a delicious leftover scone with jam and cream.

Life coaching, I have decided before trying it, is going to be more fun than therapy, which was fascinating but not always fun. I'm a big fan of life coaching already, having become addicted to many American life coaches' podcasts. From these, I have learned the difference – in theory, at least – between coaching and psychotherapy. Therapy is focused on analysing and healing past pain. Life coaching, by contrast, seems to be much more forward-looking and definitely more jolly. It's all about getting the results you want in the best of all possible futures. Which is ideal for my predicament, because my problem isn't a lack of happiness. It's the opposite, in fact. Here is how my conversation with Katherine goes after she asks me what I need help with.

Me: Um … I think I might be too happy.

Her: Too happy?

Me: Yes. But in a way that could be a problem.

Her: Can you—

Me: Yeah, I'll explain. I've always had a happy temperament, just naturally. I wake up feeling extremely happy every day, unless there's a specific upsetting problem. But that's not often, so I'm basically happy most of the time. Even when there's a problem, I'm so good at deciding that it's a mild or easily solved problem and making myself happy again that … I suppose what I'm saying is, I reckon I have some serious problems that I'm in danger of never solving because I'm happy in spite of them. So I don't suffer enough, which means I don't address the issues.

Her: Tell me about the serious problems.

Me: The main one is that I'm too busy and pressured. I mean … *incredibly* busy and pressured. All the time.

Her: What kind of busy? Work? Family commitments?

Me: Mainly work. Everything else is manageable, or it would be if it wasn't for work.

Her: What's your job?

Me: I'm a writer. I write contemporary crime novels, psychological thrillers. And I also write … have you heard of Agatha Christie's famous Belgian detective, Hercule Poirot?

Her: Of course.

Me: Well, for the past few years I've been writing new Hercule Poirot novels as well as my other crime novels. And recently, I agreed to a teaching gig that was too tempting and exciting to turn down, and I'm about to launch a coaching programme for writers, and I've co-written two murder mystery musicals and toured one of them around literary festivals, and there's a lot more of that coming up … And, I mean, I absolutely love doing all these things. That's why I do them all. I keep saying yes to new, exciting projects, and I'm really happy to be doing them. *And* I make sure I spend lots of time with my family, just hanging out, and doing the things I love doing, like swimming, seeing friends, reading, watching movies.

Her: It all sounds great to me. Are you sure there's a problem?

Me: I mean … not entirely, but I think there is, yes.

Her: What is it, then? You say you have time for your family and for relaxing …

Me: Yes. I've never been willing to sacrifice the rest of my life, no matter how much I love my work.

Her: I'm still not clear what the problem is.

Shit. Is it possible that I don't have a problem? Am I a fraud, wasting the time of a life coach who could be helping someone in greater need of her services? No, no. Calm down. There's definitely a problem. I'm not on this Skype call under false pretences.

Me: It's easiest to describe if I give you specific examples. Like … the other day, I was properly, genuinely pleased when I worked out a way of washing my face and brushing my teeth at the same time. I saved between seven and ten seconds by thinking of them as one process instead of two and washing my face *around my toothbrush.*

Her: Okay …

Me: I thought, 'Amazing! I've saved ten seconds.' Then I opened my wardrobe to find clothes to put on – I was going to do a talk at a literary lunch that day – and all my clothes were mixed up and crammed into my wardrobe in a chaotic way. I don't have time to sort out my clothes, buy new ones, throw away old ones. Those things are neither work nor fun, so I never do them. I knew I had at least three tops and two pairs of trousers that would be ideal for the literary lunch, but I couldn't see them because of the wardrobe chaos. They were probably in the laundry room, but that's in the basement – two flights down, too far away. You must think it sounds crazy: someone who doesn't have time to go to her own laundry room, who gets stressed even thinking about it, and so picks a totally unsuitable outfit for a literary lunch just because it's the one that happens to fall out of the cupboard.

Her: It does sound a little strange. But this was only one day, right?

Me: No! I never have enough time to go to the laundry room. At least three times a week I realise I haven't seen this or that garment for months or years, and I consider going down to the basement to look for it, but there's always a pressing deadline I'd miss if I did: for a podcast episode, an interview, an article, a conference call. Always something. Anyway, when I looked in my wardrobe and saw no clothes I could easily reach and wanted to wear, my heart started to beat faster. In situations like that – and more than half of each day is like that for me, with time marching on and all the things I need to do piling up in my brain – I go into my race-against-the-clock mentality, which would make sense if I was someone who, I don't know, worked in a counter-terrorism unit, whose job was to defuse bombs or something. But I'm a writer! My life shouldn't be like this. I know it shouldn't. Looking into my wardrobe that morning, I could feel the frustration set in as my regained-time advantage drained away. I actually thought, 'Fuck, now I'm going to lose the ten seconds I saved by merging face-washing and teeth-brushing into one task instead of two.' I spend a lot of my life feeling like that guy from *The Bourne Identity* who has to keep running all the time or else he might die.

Her: Why would it matter if you took a few more minutes to get dressed?

Me: Because in order to stay afloat with all the things I've committed to do – all the things I really want to do – I have to do a certain number of tasks every day, and it's more tasks than I can do in a day unless I'm constantly trying to save minutes and seconds. Unless I'm in *Bourne Identity* mode. My life has been like this for so long, it's become my automatic way of being.

Her: All right. Then I agree, you have a problem.

Shit. An American life coach with bouncy hair and bright white teeth and walls thinks I have a problem.

This is terrible. I feel worse, because now my problem is official – made so by a well-being professional – and I have no time to solve it.

Still, there's always an upside: it's nice to be proved right.

Me: Thank you! After I got dressed, in clothes that were totally unsuitable and that I didn't want to wear, I went to walk downstairs and at the top of the stairs, do you know what thoughts were running through my head? 'What planning can I do on my way down the stairs that will save me time when I get to the ground floor? I'm starving, but my train leaves in fifteen minutes and the station is six minutes' walk away. Is there any way I can make scrambled eggs at the same time as putting my laptop and charger in my bag?'

Her: That sounds very stressful.

Me: It was. It *is*. My life is, and I can feel it not doing me any good. When I'm in non-work mode, watching telly with the family or swimming, I'm not like that at all. But the rest of the time is *all* like that.

Her: All high-adrenaline running around, full of stressed-out energy?

Me: Yup. When I finish talking to you, after our hour is up, it'll be eleven o'clock UK time, and I won't be able to go to bed and sleep. I have to finish two things and hand them in by nine tomorrow morning. Then I'll have to rewrite my to-do list again, because, as happens every day, I haven't done half the things that were on it because I ran out of time.

Her: I have trouble believing that you're as happy as you say you are, when you're so overloaded with work. That sounds like an impossibly pressured life. You said you spend lots of time with your family, relaxing – are you sure that's true?

Me: Yes. Every day, between 6.30 p.m. and 10.30 p.m., I'm with my family, not working. But then when they all go to bed, I do between two and five hours more work to catch up. And I resent having to live in this ridiculous way, so I do quite a lot of skiving off, to escape the tyranny.

Her: Tyranny?

Me: Yes, that's what it feels like. I feel really tyrannised by the amount of work I have to do and the time I have in which to do it. And then the deadlines get closer, and I feel even more oppressed and tyrannised. And I genuinely want to do each individual thing! I love all of it. I just feel as if I need an extra, I don't know, seven years or so in order to do all these things in the best and happiest way, without all this second-saving, heart-pounding pressure.

Her: Do you sometimes make yourself ill by working too hard?

Me: No, not often. I'm really good in high-pressure situations. But I also think it's quite possible that I could have a breakdown tomorrow. I mean, why wouldn't I? Sometimes I'll be chatting to my mum and she'll say something quite innocent like, 'Do you want me to post that for you? I can easily nip to the post office tomorrow.' And I can barely wrap my mind round the implausible fact that *I have a very close relative who can easily nip to the post office.* I find myself thinking, 'That free-and-easy lifestyle must be possible for me too. If she can have that kind of life, then so can I.' But I don't have it – not yet. None of my days, ever, contain a spare five minutes for post-office-nipping, and I live approximately forty footsteps from my nearest post office. If I want to go there, I have to enter it as an item on my schedule, with a precise amount of time allocated to it.

Her: Could there be a really simple solution to all of this?

Me: There is. I need to take on less work. Commit to doing fewer things, stop putting so much in my schedule. I know that. I'm an enthusiast with lots of energy and an unrealistic belief in my ability to beat the odds with regard to how much work can be done in how little time. I need to plan more realistically, look after myself better and do less.

Her: Okay, great. So you have a problem and you have a solution.

Me: I can take on less from now on, and I will in future, but that doesn't help me in the short to medium term because …

At this point I break off. I can't bring myself to tell her that I'm over-committed and over-scheduled until the end of 2021.

Me: I have lots of things to write and deliver that I've already committed to, and … obviously I could write to various people and say, 'Sorry, I'm not going to be able to do this after all.' But I don't want to. I want to do everything I've planned to, but I also want to be able to enjoy my leisure time and family time, and lately I've been feeling almost as if my work is stalking me when I'm trying to relax. It's always there, crouching on top of my brain, lurking in the shadows like an oppressive—

Her: Tyrant?

Me: I was going to say 'Stalker'. But yes. Tyrannical stalker.

Her: Yet you say you're happy.

Me: Yes. I'm *very* happy. There is one small blight on my happiness, which is what we've been discussing. It doesn't make me unhappy, but I'd like to solve the problem. I want to get rid of this feeling that my work is kind of …

taunting and bullying me even during my non-working hours, and I don't want to remove it by cancelling any of my commitments. I never used to feel this way.

Her: You can easily remove the negative feelings you're having, without cancelling anything.

Me: I can? How?

Her: If you didn't feel stressed, oppressed, tyrannised, bullied and stalked by your work commitments, would you be perfectly happy?

Me: Yes! I really would.

Her: Then you easily can be.

Me: How? How do I solve the problem? Because – and I *am* happy in spite of it, I really am – but I have a strong sense that if I don't solve the problem, some big unhappiness might be coming my way at some point fairly soonish. That's just a hunch, but … it's there.

Her: Do you know that you don't ever have to change your circumstances in order to feel better or happier?

Me: Oh! Yes, I mean, kind of. I listen to lots
of life-coaching podcasts, so I know that our
feelings are caused by our thoughts, not by our
external circumstances, but –

Her: Yes. And all of our thoughts are optional.
Always. You are choosing to think that your
work commitments are stalking you and
oppressing you. You needn't think any of that.

Me: Oh, my God. Are you saying—

Her: If you dropped that thought – that belief
that your work is a tyrant, bullying you – how
would you feel? If you didn't believe that *at all*?
If you thought instead, 'I have plenty of time
for everything I want to do. There's no pressure.
There's no rush.'

Me: I can't believe I've heard this mentioned
so many times on life-coaching podcasts,
but I've never thought to apply it to my own
situation. I thought—

Her: You thought it was just the truth, right?
It's an objective fact that you don't have
enough hours in the day? It's an objective fact

that your work's oppressing you and stalking you, even during your leisure time?

Me: Yes! I didn't even think to question it.

Her: Well, you should, because it's not the truth. It's just a story you're telling yourself and you're choosing to believe it. If you want to be happier than you are now, and solve your problem, nothing needs to change about your life situation. Only your thoughts need to change. Choose new thoughts: 'In future I might commit to fewer projects, but for now, I'll pursue all my projects happily, unhurriedly, and knowing that I always have enough time. My work isn't a problem. I have no problems.' If you practise thinking thoughts like that, you'll be fuelled by a calmer energy. You'll feel less stressed, *and* be able to get more done. Then you'll understand on a deeper level – through experience, which is the best teacher – what you only understand intellectually now: none of us have any problems that we don't create with our own thoughts. Changing your thoughts solves everything, always.

Listening to her say this with such conviction, I feel a sudden movement in my brain – like a dragging followed by a pop, then a sensation of something dissolving. Then spinning. When my mind settles, I feel lighter and want to giggle. I think, 'It can't be that simple.' This is almost exactly how I feel when I reach the end of a brilliant crime novel and experience that moment of 'Oh, wow – that's it! How could it be so simple and right, and yet I didn't see it at all?'

Can it be as simple as Katherine says it is? Just change my thoughts about my situation, without changing my actual situation? I already feel much more cheerful about the work I have to do before I go to sleep tonight. I have plenty of time. I'm not even that tired.

Two hours later, I've done the two pieces of work that are due in by nine tomorrow morning – unhurriedly and without resentment. As I worked, I understood, thanks to Katherine, that I was only doing these things because I wanted to, because I'd chosen to. No one and nothing is tyrannising me. How stupid of me to have allowed that belief to set up camp in my mind, like a little Mr Brocklehurst from *Jane Eyre*, sadistically trying to make me feel as bad as possible. It was my thoughts about the work that were the oppressive stalker-tyrants, not the work itself. My work is amazing. I love it. And if I don't love my Mr Brocklehurst thoughts, I can change them. I already have.

Have I just discovered the one and only secret of how to be perfectly happy forever?

2

My Happiness Hunches – the Longlist

I was born in Manchester, and spent all but one of the first 38 years of my life living in the north of England. I moved to Cambridge in 2010 and have lived there and in the Cotswolds since, but there's still quite a lot of Northern in me – 38 years' worth, to be precise – as I realise when, seconds after wondering if my session with Katherine has led me to discover the all-powerful, everlasting secret of happiness, a sarcastic voice in my head mutters, 'Give over, for God's sake.'

It *cannot* be as simple as that.

Yet Katherine has assured me that it is.

Nope. Sorry. Nothing is that straightforward. I can't bring myself to believe that a question that baffled Plato and Aristotle … Wait, did it? I have no idea and just made that up. It must have, surely. Katherine would insist that this was a thought and not a fact, but let's go with it for the time being. I can't believe that a mystery that foxed Plato, Aristotle and other ancient wise men who get made into statues has just been definitively solved by Katherine the American life coach.

On the other hand, I've read the complete works of Agatha Christie more than four times, so I ought to have learned by now that whenever you think, 'No way – that unlikely person *cannot* be the one', they very often are.

Here's the thing: I *did* feel immediately brilliant, unstalked and unoppressed as I did my late-night work after talking to Katherine, but … if I can change my thoughts, delete the Mr Brocklehurst-ish ones and feel happy at will, that might make me believe that my current work patterns are fine. And … I don't think they are. I don't think they're good for me.

Wait. That's just a thought too. It might not be true. And does happiness mean nothing more than feeling as good as you can in each moment? Doesn't it also mean feeling happy that you're taking care of your long-term well-being, sanity and health? Well-being is a different thing from happiness, of course. I think so, anyway.

Actually, I have no idea what I'm talking about.

Suddenly, it becomes important – urgent, even – that I should find out what happiness means. In a few months, I am planning to launch a coaching programme that's designed to help writers of every kind, from beginners to established bestsellers, withstand the many psychological and emotional challenges that come with being a writer. How can I do this without knowing what happiness and well-being are, and how to bring more of both into a person's life? I thought I knew, but now Katherine has turned everything on its head. If our suboptimal thoughts are the only thing standing between us and complete, perfect happiness …

But what if that's a load of nonsense? (Any thoughts, dear sidekick?)

Right, that's it. I have to solve this puzzle. It won't be the first real-life mystery I've investigated. Still, this happiness mystery is of a very different kind to anything I've tackled before. It's probably going to be harder to solve. Luckily, I love a challenge.

Before I do any on-the-ground sleuthing of my own, I need to buy and read all the literature I can find on the subject. With great efficiency and enthusiasm, I order the following books:

The Courage Habit
by Kate Swoboda

Self Coaching 101
by Brooke Castillo

The Happiness Project
by Gretchen Rubin

Finding Your Own North Star
by Martha Beck

The Art of Happiness
by the Dalai Lama

The Pursuit of Happiness
by Ruth Whippman

Help Me! One Woman's Quest to Find Out if Self-Help Really Can Change Her Life
by Marianne Power

How Emotions Are Made
by Lisa Feldman Barrett

Stumbling on Happiness
by Daniel Gilbert

The Ultimate Happiness Prescription
by Deepak Chopra

Smile or Die
by Barbara Ehrenreich

Flow: The Psychology of Happiness
by Mihaly Csikszentmihalyi

The Happiness Advantage
by Shawn Achor

Loving What Is
by Byron Katie

Joyful
by Ingrid Fetell Lee

The 5 AM Club
by Robin Sharma

Happy: Why More or Less Everything is Absolutely Fine
by Derren Brown

I determinedly ignore the fact that I seem to be embarking upon yet another project less than two days after I told a life coach that I feel stalked by my workload and commitments.

Felt. It's not how I feel any more, right? Because I changed my thoughts, and I now believe that I have plenty of time for everything I want to do. I love buying books; it makes me happy. And if the thought of committing to reading every single book I've just bought is threatening to bring back that Mr Brocklehurst feeling, then I can think a new thought: 'I will read as many of them as I fancy reading, and I'll decide that's enough, and be satisfied with that result.'

Sorted.

So, which one will I read first? And when, given that I—

Change that thought. Plenty of time.

Wait. None of the books in my newly ordered, soon-to-arrive pile are by Plato or Aristotle, or even Émile Durkheim, whose name I dimly remember from a cobwebby corner of my sociology A-level syllabus. Didn't Durkheim say something about how working in the wrong way makes people unhappy? Are there enough ancient, statue-y writers among the books I've ordered? Probably not.

Also, as soon as I start reading other people's happiness theories, I'm going to be swayed. Possibly back and forth and round and about, dozens of times. I am one of the most easily swayed people on the planet.

This isn't a problem – I like being swayed, I enjoy seeking out new things to believe in wholeheartedly, and I love it when I stumble upon a brilliantly expressed argument that completely changes my mind about something.

If this is about to happen to me as I investigate the mystery of happiness, I should jot down some of my own un-influenced thoughts first. In crime fiction, detectives often form wild, unsubstantiated theories before they've had a chance to do much sleuthing, and their sidekicks caution them, saying, 'But you have no way of knowing that!' Part of the suspense comes from wondering if their intuitive hunches will turn out to be correct.

I want to take stock of my own thoughts and intuitions on the subject first, before immersing myself in the thoughts of experts. Then, once I've consulted the case files so far and found out all I can, I shall revisit my own hypotheses and see if I've changed my mind, see if the evidence I've gathered has led me to a solution far better and more satisfying than my initial theories.

What are my happiness hunches? I have many. How will they stand up against the philosophies of the big boys?

(Sorry, Katherine. You've already given me a flawless solution to the mystery, and here I am wanting to try out some alternative hypotheses. Oh me of little faith! Also, what if there are no 'big boys'? I can choose to believe that my opinions about happiness are every bit as important as Aristotle's or Plato's. And I can choose not to care if every university philosophy department in the world disagrees with me about that. Wow. I really love this way of looking at life. It is actually making me incredibly happy.)

The important thing, at this early stage in my investigation, is not to censor myself when listing my insights and tentative theories. I grab a notebook and a pen and start to write.

My list looks like this, except in terrible handwriting:

Happiness Hunches

1. Differences Between Things
2. Bad Advice = Good
3. The Cancellation
4. NEAs
5. What if it IS my job?
6. The Positive in the Negative (Grudges)
7. The 65 Days (Eligible? Yes! Why not?)

That's it. I don't make any further, clarifying notes. There's no need. I know exactly what I mean by each item. No one else does yet – not even you, dear side-kick, but that's fine. I'll share all relevant information with you in due course, I promise. I'm not ready to discuss my theories yet, as Poirot so often says early in his investigations.

This is a mystery, after all. I want to play fair and give you all the clues I can.

And now, it's time to open the old case files and see what the big boys had to say …

3

The Case File So Far

Wow. I don't think I was quite prepared for how many big boys there are in the happiness field. Too many, in fact, to list them all, so in the selection below I've included the ones that struck me as having, potentially, the highest happiness clue-count – in other words, the ones that might prove the most helpful in solving our happiness mystery.

To make this fun (as well as instructive; that's important too), let's choose our favourite theories of happiness from this list. I'll give you the run-down first, then I'll give you a chance to choose. Finally, I'll tell you which of these big-boy theories I like best.

No. 15: Socrates

Socrates believed that happiness is a pursuable and achievable goal, rather than a gift bestowed at the gods' discretion. He made a distinction between fleeting pleasure and true happiness, which he saw as an enduring reward for living well. Here's my favourite part: he thought that, although it might seem as though the fulfilment of our desires is what makes us happy, we can only reach true happiness if, once obtained or achieved, we use the object of our desire well. Money, for example, can be used badly: wasted, spent on things that aren't good for us or on immoral things. Only by way of wisdom – critical thought and reflection – which Socrates believed to be necessary in order to bring out the very best of human nature – can money make us happy.

Socrates argued that if the objects of our desire *do* make us happy, it is not they themselves that have caused the happy state but rather our wisdom in relation to them. His emphasis was on our own agency and choices and, in particular, our wisdom; he did not believe that external events could make us happy or unhappy.

Socrates practised what he preached, it seems. He maintained his wise and happy state of inner peace even when facing execution for shunning the gods and corrupting the young, and he remained upbeat and chatty right up until he drank the hemlock that killed him.

No. 14: Plato

The ancient Greeks had a word for happiness: *eudaimona*. In fact, this is too easy a translation. To define it in English as 'happiness' doesn't quite get to the crux of the meaning. 'Eu' means good, and 'daimon' means soul or self, so the word might be more accurately understood to mean a realisation of purpose. By this definition, a happy person might be someone who has lived up to her potential, made her life meaningful and so achieved her true and perfect form.

In *The Republic*, Plato offers the recipe for this self-actualisation: the development of the four cardinal virtues of wisdom, temperance, courage and justice. He believes it is necessary to have '*arete*' (excellence) in these areas in order to achieve happiness, and that happiness is bound up with morality and reachable only by the virtuous.

No. 13: Aristotle

Aristotle believed that happiness is to be found in the fulfilment of our nature. That which makes us specifically human and differentiates us from animals, he said, is our capacity for reason, and it's this uniquely human quality that must be perfected in order for us to be the best versions of ourselves. He believed that we don't need to quash the characteristics we share with animals – the seeking of pleasure – but that we should find ways to tame them into aiding our greater and more noble goals.

For those who are not naturally possessed of a virtuous character but would nevertheless like to achieve happiness ('LOL! Me', as my teenage daughter would say), Aristotle recommends finding the balance between excess and deficiency, the 'golden mean'. For example, if you're at the centre point of the scale that has hot-headed at one extreme and cowardly at the other, then you're probably courageous. Aristotle argued that the intellectual exercise of finding the mean in this way can help you to develop a good character, and then, once you're sufficiently trained, making the right, reason-based choices becomes your go-to position and you're well on your way to a happy life.

No 12: Marcus Aurelius (Stoicism)

The reign of Marcus Aurelius, emperor of Rome from AD 161 to 180, coincided with war, rebellion and the

Antonine Plague, which killed five million people. Perhaps it's no surprise, then, that he believed that 'Our life is what our thoughts make it'; you can see how that might have seemed like an indispensable coping tool, given what he had to contend with.

Although it is thought that his writings, in which he describes his Stoic practices, were a personal exercise and not intended for publication, his *Meditations* reads like a way-ahead-of-its-time self-help book on how to be happy. Stoicism advocates the acceptance of whatever circumstance we find ourselves in, and makes it our own responsibility (and no one else's) to create our happiness with our minds, no matter what our life situation might be – because our minds are the only things over which we have power.

Marcus Aurelius believed that circumstances are never innately positive or negative, and are only made 'good' or 'bad' by the way we think about them; we can choose to react with composure and calmness to whatever comes our way, and it's in this strength and freedom that happiness can be found.

No. 11: Thomas Aquinas

A thirteenth-century Dominican friar, Aquinas managed to unite the seemingly at odds ancient Greek eudaimonism with Christian theology by describing the idea of two distinct yet connected understandings of happiness. In Aquinas's theory, 'happiness' is the definitive goal of every human, and the yearning for it is the drive behind every action taken. On the question of 'What will make us happy?', Aquinas rules out many possible answers – possessions, status, physical pleasure, even virtues such as knowledge and wisdom – on the grounds that dissatisfaction and suffering are found even once these have been attained. We might feel enjoyment upon acquiring such things, but it's a fleeting pleasure and so cannot be perfect happiness.

Aquinas believed that there were two types of happiness: *felicitas* and *beatitudo*. Felicitas is imperfect happiness and can be achieved in this life by cultivating values such as wisdom, courage, moderation and justice. Beatitudo is the ultimate form of happiness and is only available to you in death, when you can know God directly. In order to be in with a chance of reaching this state of eternal bliss you need to focus on the theological virtues of faith, hope and love. Aquinas's theology, then, is not concerned with obedience and piety for its own sake, but as steps you can take towards achieving perfect happiness for yourself.

No. 10: Al-Ghazali

Like Thomas Aquinas, twelfth-century philosopher, theologian and mystic al-Ghazali believed that both faith and reason were essential to happiness and that, of the two, faith would always be supreme. The first step to achieving happiness, he said, is to realise that we are first and foremost spiritual beings. Al-Ghazali wanted to offer a way to God that didn't rely on adherence to the rules of Islam. Imagination and mysticism, not reason and logic, were, according to him, the better routes to truth and happiness.

Al-Ghazali believed that humans experience pain as a result of being born in a state of disconnection from the Ultimate Reality. In an attempt to relieve this hurt, we fruitlessly pursue transient physical pleasures and try to heal a spiritual pain by physical means, which can only cause us further unhappiness. For al-Ghazali, the self is perfect but becomes obscured by passions and desires. Happiest are those who can rid themselves of these obstructions.

No. 9: René Descartes

The sixteenth-century philosopher, mathematician and scientist René Descartes equated happiness with the attainment of wisdom. For him, a happy life was found in the practice of philosophy, which he saw as medicine for the brain. A happy person, he believed, would enjoy psychological contentment and tranquillity as the result of a well-ordered mind.

Descartes argued that mental illness, though common, is very difficult to detect, as it is impossible for us to know if our minds are healthy and working as they should be. He believed that happiness is achievable in this life, and saw no need to seek any sort of supernatural bliss. He thought it was possible to weather pain and suffering and remain happy, suggesting that we can distract ourselves from mental pain by spending time 'in the consideration of objects which could furnish contentment and joy'. This approach worked for him: he believed that his tendency towards optimism cured him of the chronic illness that his doctors had been convinced would kill him.

No. 8 Jeremy Bentham

Happiness was at the centre of the moral universe for nineteenth-century philosopher and social reformer Jeremy Bentham. Observing that the avoidance of pain and the pursuit of pleasure were the fundamental motivators behind all of our actions, Bentham concluded that we are governed by these two 'sovereign masters' in the same way that nature is subject to the laws of physics. Happiness for Bentham was a predominance of pleasure over pain. He was the founding father of utilitarianism, a doctrine that evaluates actions purely on their consequences and asserts that happiness is the sole criterion by which we can judge what is right and wrong.

Pleasure and pain, he argued, are quantifiable by the method of 'hedonic calculus', and only by measuring the pleasure or pain caused by actions can we determine which is the right action to take. He therefore believed that whatever action leads to the greatest happiness for the largest number of people, both immediately and as time goes on, must also be the most moral action.

Bentham did not value one sort of happiness over another, and made no distinction between the 'high' satisfactions of the mind and the 'low' pleasures of the body, a position that possibly led to his protégé John Stuart Mill clarifying his own stance, which was that it is definitely objectively better to be an unhappy human being than a 'satisfied pig', and that a cheesed-off Socrates still has more intrinsic value than a jolly fool.

No. 7: Immanuel Kant

The Prussian philosopher said: 'Morality is not properly the doctrine of how we may make ourselves happy, but how we may make ourselves worthy of happiness.'[1] He believed that pursuing happiness would not lead to finding happiness, and therefore seeking our own happiness can't be the main moral mission of humanity. More important was producing 'a will that is good', which he acknowledges might limit our ability to achieve personal happiness in some respects. In Kant's view, well-being and good conduct do not always go hand in hand, and seeking one's own happiness often prevents correct moral behaviour. He wrote: 'Every admixture of incentives taken from one's own happiness is a hindrance to providing the moral law with influence on the human heart.'[2]

Of all the big boys, Kant seems to be the most opposed to the pursuit of happiness, arguing that to seek our own pleasure and well-being is to tell virtue 'to her face that it is not her beauty but only our advantage that attaches us to her'.[3]

---

1. Immanuel Kant, *Critique of Pure Reason*
2. Immanuel Kant, *Critique of Practical Reason*
3. Immanuel Kant, *Groundwork of the Metaphysics of Morals*

No. 6: Arthur Schopenhauer

The nineteenth-century German philosopher is renowned for his pessimistic view of life as defined by needless suffering. He didn't believe that permanent or lasting happiness was possible, and thought that the best we could hope for was to minimise our pain. He said:

> We must set limits to our wishes, curb our desires, moderate our anger, always remembering that an individual can attain only an infinitesimal share in anything that is worth having; and that, on the other hand, everyone must incur many of the ills of life ... and if we fail to observe this rule, no position of wealth or power will prevent us from feeling wretched.[4]

Schopenhauer believed that our personality type, or character disposition, is extremely important in determining how happy we will be throughout our lives. He was an advocate of solitude as a means of minimising suffering. The compromises involved in spending time with other people, he thought, were not worth making. In his opinion, people are untrustworthy, and friendship is usually nothing more than self-interest. The company of others, he

---

4. Arthur Schopenhauer, *Essays and Aphorisms*, Section 16

believed, makes it impossible for us to be our true selves, and there are not enough advantages to human relationships to compensate us for this loss of true self-expression. Schopenhauer believed that talented people especially should avoid their fellow humans and choose solitude.

No. 5: Bertrand Russell

Unlike Schopenhauer, Bertrand Russell was an optimist. He stressed the importance of 'zest' in relation to happiness, and defined this as an 'appetite for possible things, upon which all happiness, whether of men or animals, ultimately depends'. He said, 'What hunger is in relation to food, zest is in relation to life.' Things that work against zest – and therefore the attainment of happiness – include, in Russell's opinion, boredom, fatigue and self-absorption. He argued that for a happy person, 'one's ego is no very large part of the world' and believed that 'a world full of happiness is not beyond human power to create. The real obstacles lie in the heart of man, and the cure for these is a firm hope.'[5]

5. All quotations here from Bertrand Russell, *The Conquest of Happiness*

No. 4: The Dalai Lama

The leader of Tibetan Buddhism wrote a handbook for living in 1998 entitled, *The Art of Happiness*. In it, he says:

> I believe that the very purpose of life is to be happy. From the very core of our being, we desire contentment. I have found that the more we care for the happiness of others, the greater is our own sense of well-being. Cultivating a close, warm-hearted feeling for others automatically puts the mind at ease. Since we are not solely material creatures, it is a mistake to place all our hopes for happiness on external development alone. The key is to develop inner peace.

No. 3: Mihaly Csikszentmihalyi

American-Hungarian psychologist Mihaly Csikszentmihalyi believes that 'flow' is the key to happiness, and wrote an influential book with that title. Flow is that in-the-zone state that creative people experience when they are fully focused on and immersed in their creative work, and lose their awareness of things that would normally enter their consciousness and possibly bother or annoy them, such as the activity going on around them, the passing of time, the need for food and water and all other physical and psychological discomforts that might otherwise intrude.

Csikszentmihalyi describes the flow state as a kind of ecstasy, in which our body and identity disappear from our consciousness, and our existence is, effectively, temporarily suspended as the activity that is consuming all of our attention takes over and we feel as if we are at one with it.

No. 2: Martin Seligman

Widely acknowledged as the founder of positive psychology, Martin Seligman's evolving theory about why happy people are happy has shifted the focus from the negative – human weaknesses and how we can repair these – to the positive: our strengths, and how we can build on them. Seligman believes that happiness has three dimensions that can be cultivated: the Pleasant Life, the Good Life, and the Meaningful Life.

Seligman does not accept that happiness is merely the elimination of misery and has also rejected the accepted tenet of psychology and psychotherapy that we need to look at a person's past in order to explain happiness or the lack thereof.

Unhappiness, he believes, is not due to how we think about the past but how we think about the future: we can be happy if only we can believe that the future will be good. Seligman's 'PERMA' model defines what elements are necessary for a happy life and outlines what we can do to exploit these to reach maximum happiness. The elements are:

Positive Emotion (gratitude, love, pleasure, optimism)

Engagement (losing yourself in an activity: playing music, sport, artistic pursuits)

Relationships (cultivate positive interactions with a range of people, seek out group activities)

Meaning (spirituality, belief in your work, volunteering for a cause, raising children)

Accomplishments (set yourself goals, put effort into achieving them).

In Seligman's opinion, the promotion of these principles will lead to happier individuals and societies.

No. 1: Anthony Seldon

The co-founder of the Action for Happiness organisation, Anthony Seldon sets out to address the fact that, despite all the advances of the modern world, unhappiness is on the rise. He believes that there are natural cures available for our depressed state and that happiness is attainable for all of us. The neuroplasticity of our brains, Seldon believes, allows us to enhance our happiness capability through training and by cultivating certain skills. He has campaigned extensively for a more holistic approach to education, in which system he believes the promotion of happiness is an absolutely crucial but sadly overlooked area. Seldon advocates happiness classes for children, and implemented these at Wellington College during his time there as head teacher. He maintains that this emphasis on happiness had a positive effect upon exam results.

Like Martin Seligman, Seldon believes that it is optimism that leads to success, not the other way around. This can be built on by training our brains to highlight our positive feelings – practise thinking about the things you are grateful for, for example, and you will feel happier. Seldon recommends that we reject pleasure-seeking in the areas of possessions, wealth, status and drink/drugs, and instead practise meditation, healthy eating and exercise. He believes that we should concentrate on nurturing our relationships, finding connection with others, learning and challenging ourselves, and making time to do the things we love. Adversity does not need to be a bar to our happiness, he argues, but can be a spark for positive change. Worry, on the other hand, only makes us self-centred and diminishes our chances of achieving happiness. Seldon argues that the promotion of happiness should be the business of individuals, but also, and equally, of educators and governments as it is 'too serious a matter to be treated as flippant any longer'.

*

Well, I don't know about you, but I'm finding it harder to pick and choose between those theories and definitions of happiness than I expected to. I adore Bertrand Russell's idea of zest, and admire Marcus Aurelius's bad-ass Stoic approach that puts one's own mind totally in charge of proceedings (he sounds very much as if he has benefited from a session with Katherine the life coach, in fact). The ancient Greeks all offer extremely wise takes on the matter, and I found myself chortling, and muttering 'Relatable!', at Schopenhauer's 'shun all people, they're a bit shit' approach – it reminds me of Professor Henry Higgins in *My Fair Lady*, whom I also love, and who had similarly disparaging views about half of the population, if not all of it. And Mihaly Csikszentmihalyi's theory of flow is fascinating too …

Hmm. I feel as if I'm further away from finding one true and conclusive definition of happiness than I've ever been. That was absolutely not what was supposed to happen.

Could it be that all of the above are correct, valid and wise definitions?

I hope not. That kind of structural twist works perfectly in *Murder on the Orient Express*, but I'm holding out for my One Right Answer. And, as so often in detective and mystery fiction, the solution towards which everything seems to point is not what the detective hoped or expected it would be. So far in my investigation, nothing I have come across has felt as real, or has given me as much of a perfect, blindsided-by-a-denouement-revelation moment, as Katherine's 'change your thoughts and be happy' prescription, which I've been practising avidly. Come to think of it, Katherine's philosophy and ethics of happiness (though she would never call it that) have much in common with Marcus Aurelius's hot take (though he would never call it that).

And, in practice, changing my thoughts has been working like a dream. I still have a lot to do (not 'too much' – that's just a thought), and I am, without doubt, exhausted – even more so now that I seem to be writing a book about happiness. Right now, for instance, as I type this, I've got a crumpled paper bag full of pastry crumbs stuffed into my bra, scratching against my skin. My dog, Brewster, would swallow it whole if I put it next to me on the desk and, although it would only take me five seconds to go and put the bag on a high shelf that he can't reach, I don't at present have five seconds to spare.

Still. I no longer feel stalked, oppressed or tyrannised by my work. When I get too tired while working, I fall asleep, wherever I am. It's great! I don't even have to decide to get into bed and try to sleep; my body makes the decision for me. And I don't need to believe that having a paper bag full of crumbs in my bra is a problem; it's my choice to think whatever I want about that feature of my present situation.

Yet still a voice in my head insists that Katherine the coach can't be right; she can't have cracked it.

Perhaps the truth is that I don't want to get my happiness-mystery solution from Aristotle, Schopenhauer or Katherine. I want to find it myself. I don't want to be helped or saved by a Poirot equivalent. I want to be the Poirot in my own life. (Only in my own life, mind. Definitely not on a screen, big or small. David Suchet, Kenneth Branagh and John Malkovich don't need to worry about competition from me.)

Wait. That's given me an idea …

4

Another Session with a Life Coach

Her name is Lyssa. Like Katherine, she's American. Our coaching call is on Zoom, not Skype, and starts with a disaster: I press the wrong key on my computer, cut off the call and we have to start again. This takes up ten minutes, throughout which I'm cursing through teeth that are simultaneously gritted and embedded in my lower lip, thinking, 'Minutes are passing! Minutes I cannot spare!'

At last we get it sorted. Lyssa and the room I can see behind her are nowhere near as life-coach-perfect as Katherine and her room were. Lyssa's room is too long and not deep enough; she might, in fact, have set up a temporary workstation in a corridor of some kind. Still, I warm to her immediately. I allow myself to decide within seconds that I prefer her. Her smile is more true-friend than friendly-professional. I can imagine her giving me a hug, whereas that never entered my mind with Katherine. I should stress that I would absolutely hate it if any American life coach tried to give me a hug, but it turns out that I still like them to look as if hugs are in their repertoire. (As I have this thought, I picture Katherine handing me an apricot gin and tonic in a crystal-studded glass, with an expression on her face that says, 'Is this not better than any hug?' I think this might be what psychologists call projection. Or just plain weirdness. One or the other.)

Lyssa asks what she can help me with today.

I wonder how much to tell her. I've booked this session because of Hercule Poirot, but I have no intention of admitting it. Thinking about all the actors who have played him over the years, and how markedly different their Poirots were, made me wonder if it's only Katherine or if all life coaches share the belief that changing your thoughts is the solution to every problem.

Since talking to Katherine and making my Happiness Hunches longlist, something has occurred to me: if we can change our thoughts about our workload and how much time we have available, surely we can do the same in relation to other people? And if that's true, if Katherine would say it was true, then I might have to disagree with her quite a lot.

That would be a relief. Agreeing too completely with anyone always makes me feel like I've failed in some obscure way.

Of course, I could have booked another session with Katherine – that being the obvious way to find out what she'd say – and maybe I will at some point, but what she wouldn't be able to tell me is whether all life coaches endorse her approach. Lyssa also won't be able to speak for her whole profession, but she's one more life coach to add to my study, or hobby, or whatever is the right name for it.

You see, something else has happened since my session with Katherine: I've become aware of just how many American life coaches are available on the internet, offering sample sessions, mini-sessions, very affordable one-off sessions. There are thousands of them out there. If I had the time (ha!) I would try all of them, the way I once tested every single perfume in every perfume-selling shop in Manchester city centre and became the north of England's leading perfume expert. Once I decide I'm interested in something, whether it's perfume, happiness, Agatha Christie or life coaching, I very quickly become obsessed.

I ask Lyssa if she believes that we can solve any problem by changing our thoughts.

Her: Absolutely. Once we change the way we think about any difficulty, our feelings and actions can't help but change. All the results we see in our lives come from our thoughts.

Me: I see what you mean, but I wonder—

Her: Let's talk about a specific problem that you've got. It's always easier if we focus in on something particular.

I tell her the same story I told Katherine: my enormous workload, the sense of oppression I felt before I changed my thoughts about it, the suspicion that, post-Katherine, I might now be in a worse situation because I'm still doing way more than is good for me, and likely to carry on doing so because I'm now thinking it's all amazing and not oppressive at all. Lyssa tells me I'm thinking about it in the wrong way.

Me: How so?

Her: Well, it's obviously going to make you feel awful if you think *that* thought.

Me: Which thought?

Her: The one you just told me you've been thinking: that maybe you're still doing too much and it's not good for you, and now that you've redefined doing too much as great, you're in a worse situation than you were in before. If that's what you're thinking, how's that going to make you feel?

Me: I actually feel fine. I always feel quite happy. This is part of the problem, as I told the last coach I spoke to.

Her: Are you sure you feel happy?

Me: Yes.

Her: But if you believe that you might be colluding in a delusion that ultimately harms you – the delusion that you're not under pressure and you have enough time and not too much work to do – that can't feel good, can it? If you truly believe you might be acting in a way that won't benefit you in the long-term? *Do* you truly believe that?

Me: I think it's a strong possibility. I mean, I'm still working until I fall asleep over my laptop at 2 a.m. most days. The other day I

drafted a round-robin email to all members of
every branch of my husband's and my family
suggesting that we don't bother with Christmas
presents this year, even for the children, because
I don't have time between now and December
even to think the word 'Christmas', let alone
do anything about it. Luckily, I saw sense and
deleted it before pressing 'send'.

Her: Sounds to me like your coaching session
with the other coach didn't work as well as you
think it did. You're still very clearly believing that
you have too much to do, and you don't sound
happy about it.

Me: No, it really did work. I *am* feeling better.
I'm just trying to describe to you the overall
situation. Like, before the coaching session, the
mention of Christmas would have made me
want to start sobbing and fake my own death
to escape the extra work. Now I feel totally fine
about it: I'll buy presents *and* wrap them, and it
will all be fine. I'll do it happily – because if I'm
going to do it, and I am, then I might as well do
it in a jolly way.

Her: And then later on you'll fall asleep at your
computer at 2 a.m.?

Me: Probably more like 3 a.m., if it's a
Christmas-chores day *and* I have to work as well.

Her: Here's what I think you're getting wrong,
and please don't beat yourself up about it,
because it's an extremely common mistake –

Me: Oh, I never beat myself up about anything.

Her: I think you're thinking, 'I have too many
work commitments and I'm under too much
pressure, and it's bound to be doing me harm,
but I want to feel happy about it rather than
miserable because then I will suffer less.'

Me: Well … no, because after speaking to the
last life coach, I know that 'too many work
commitments' and 'too much pressure' are just
thoughts I've made up in my brain. They're not
facts, so I don't need to believe them and feel
oppressed and overwhelmed accordingly.

Her: Here's the thing, Sophie. That's a very *clever*
answer—

Me: Thank you.

Her: But you're not being honest.

Me: Oh.

Her: You're saying they're only thoughts and not facts, but it's clear to me that, whatever you *say*, you do believe that it's an objective fact that you have too much to do and that your life contains an intolerable amount of pressure.

Me: (after a long pause) Yes, I think you're right. I think … I *do* still believe that, and the reason I feel so much better since I talked to the other coach is that I totally understand that it's just a belief in my brain, and that it's possible to believe something that's less depressing. If I'm going to be *doing* all the work, which I am, then I might as well think, 'I've chosen to do all this, and it all matters to me, and I could cancel it all if I wanted to, which I don't – and so I'm just going to do what I can every day and enjoy the process.'

Her: Right. You feel better than you did before because you understand intellectually that thoughts aren't facts. You believe that you can change your thoughts, and so you feel more empowered.

Me: Right.

Her: The problem is that you think you've
changed your thoughts and succeeded in
thinking positively about a situation that is
inherently negative.

Me: Well—

Her: Can I tell you how I know that? Because
you *do* feel happier – less stalked and bullied
by your work, as you said – so we know that
the thinking positive part is working. At the
same time, you're worried that this new happy
attitude might be doing you harm because your
circumstances remain the same. The amount of
work you have to do remains the same. So, your
worry that being happy about it is harmful to
you is all the evidence I need in order to know
that you believe your circumstances are negative,
and not something you should be happy about.

Me: I suppose that's true, yes. Yes! Which means
I haven't really changed my thoughts! That's why
I'm still worrying, at some level. I'm trying to
think positively about a negative situation, when
I should be trying to believe that there's nothing
negative about the situation.

I can see my mistake very clearly. It's not Katherine's fault, either. It's a result of me wanting to give myself a gold star for the brilliant achievement of changing my thoughts when in fact I'd only changed the top-layer.

> Me: If I truly believed that work was just work and I didn't have words in my brain like 'too much' and 'stress' –

> Her: But, Sophie, the important thing is not to believe in every situation that everything is perfect. Sometimes you might choose to say, 'This is not what I want and it's not good for me.' Sometimes the right thing for us is to choose to think a thought that's kind of positive *and* negative at the same time – a thought like, 'I don't want my life to be like this any more, and so I'm going to make some changes.' And then that thought empowers us to make some great transformations and up-level ourselves and our lives. The important thing is to realise that *you can and should always choose to believe what it serves you best to believe.*

> Me: Right. I think I totally get this now. And the reason I want to think happy thoughts about my current workload, and my commitments for the

next year or so, is that I have no choice but to do that work, so—

Her: That's not true. We always have a choice.

Me: True. I mean, I'm not willing to allow myself the option of not doing the work I've promised to do.

Her: Okay. So you choose to honour your commitments.

Me: I do. So, I should just do the work and feel happy about it, right? And unstressed.

Her: I wonder. Is there a more important commitment you should have made a while back, and that you should be honouring?

Me: What do you mean?

Her: A commitment to yourself, maybe? To take care of yourself and not stretch yourself to breaking point? Can I tell you what I think might be going on here? I don't mean to be confronting, but—

Me: Confront away, please!

Her: Could it be that you're wanting to feel good about yourself, so you tell yourself you're honouring your work commitments to other people, and you try to do that – and at the same time you're neglecting everything that you owe to yourself?

Me: Um … yes, that actually sounds quite likely. Why would I do that?

Her: It's very common. It's usually rooted either in a belief that other people matter more than you do – that's the people-pleasing part of it – or there could also be an element of perfectionism, the over-achiever's Achilles heel: you can't think well of yourself unless you're over-achieving, so you take on too much, try to do it all perfectly and wear yourself out.

Me: Yes! I am both of those unfortunate things, for sure.

Her: Sophie, what if I were to say to you that I think you should take responsibility right now for your long-term health and happiness?

Me: I'd agree with you.

Her: Cancel half of your work commitments –

Me: Steady on.

Her: What's the worst-case scenario? Some people would be angry and disappointed? You'd earn less money? So what?

Me: You're right. That is absolutely what I should do. But I'm not going to.

Her: And that's because of a thought you're having that I doubt you're even aware of. It probably begins with the words, 'It would be the end of the world if I cancelled anything because …'

Me: I know it wouldn't be the end of the world.

Her: Intellectually you know it, but you don't truly know it. Deep down, in the part of us that's buried beneath the rational, we all believe all kinds of crazy shit. We have thoughts in that part of us that are so much more powerful and convincing than the ones we believe with our rational, presentable brains.

Me: I agree one hundred per cent. That's why I love Iris Murdoch's novels. Have you read Iris Murdoch?

Her: I have not.

Me: I think my deep-down thought is something like, 'It would be the end of the world if I cancelled anything because … then I'd have to face up to or confront something I'd really rather not.'

Her: I agree absolutely.

Me: And … I've no idea what that thing might be, which is quite exciting!

Her: You're not afraid to probe more deeply and maybe find out what it is you're avoiding?

Me: No! I love a good mystery and I love solving mysteries – any mystery, no matter what the solution turns out to be.

Her: Well … that is actually a very healthy attitude to take to one's personal growth!

We grin at each other. You could call it a British hug. That's how I'm choosing to think of it.

> Me: Wait. Can we talk about your thoughts and beliefs for a minute? At the beginning of our conversation, you said that all the results we see in our lives come from our thoughts.

> Her: It's true.

> Me: But … it isn't. If a hurricane blows the roof off my house, it's not my thoughts that have caused the result of a roofless house.

> Her: Nope. That's the hurricane that's caused that. Sophie, our session's nearly finished. If you'd like to book another—

> Me: Can I ask you one more question? Do *you* think, from everything I've told you, that I've taken on too much? Too many work commitments?

> Her: I do, yes.

> Me: But … isn't 'too much work' just a thought and not a fact?

Her: Well, yes, the value judgement 'too much' is a thought for sure. But the facts – unarguable in a court of law – are that you have committed to do this piece of work and that piece of work and those other pieces of work. Right?

Me: Yup.

Her: And you only have twenty-four hours in each day, like the rest of us, and you need to spend some of those hours sleeping.

Me: Yes, or I'll die. You're right. The last coach I spoke to didn't say facts don't exist.

This is turning out to be more complicated than I thought. Thoughts are not the be-all and end-all; facts also have to be taken into account.

Wait. Didn't Katherine say that my life sounded 'impossibly pressured' or words to that effect? I'm sure she did. So maybe she and Lyssa agree on the facts of the case. Thinking back to our conversation, I'm pretty sure Katherine wasn't trying to say, 'Just think differently and don't cancel anything.' Perhaps Katherine's position could be more accurately sum-marised as: 'If you're not willing to decrease your workload, then you should think about it differently, because it's not going to help you to think of it as a tyrannical, oppressive stalker.'

Lyssa took it one step further. Her advice can be summarised like this: 'If you're not willing to decrease your workload, then that unwillingness is caused by a thought, and *that's* the thought you should work on changing – because you really need to take better care of yourself.'

Her: So, Sophie, that's the end of our free mini-session. Would you like to book another session?

Me: Definitely. Yes.

As we arrange our next Zoom call, I feel a pang of guilt. Katherine – my first, my original, provider of my eureka moment – asked me the same question and I said no. Why? And why did Lyssa get a 'yes'? Is it because she seems so biased in favour of me doing less work? Or because my session with Katherine – providing the One True Answer, as I believed it did at the time – felt so perfect and complete?

One reason I want to talk to Lyssa again is that I haven't asked her the main question I wanted to ask her about other people and how their behaviour fits into the thoughts/facts philosophy. Actually, I'd like to know what Katherine thinks about that too. Most of all, I'd love to hear Katherine's thoughts about Lyssa's opinion of my work situation.

Can it do any harm to book second sessions with *two* life coaches?

Of course not. That's not even a question worth considering. I have plenty of time for chatting to life coaches. And while I wait, I can read books by different life coaches – the ones I ordered online and which have now arrived.

I'm convinced I'm on the right path. This is how I'm going to find the solution to the happiness mystery.

5

The Books (and
the Podcasts)

I'd better confess at this point that I have a long-standing relationship with the self-help industry. And ... you know all those strange and varied New Age things you might think of as tangentially connected to the self-help industry? Reiki, homeopathy, acupuncture, Bright Path Ascension meditation, crystal healing, chakra balancing – I've tried them all. What did I think of them? Did they work? Honestly, I have no idea. Talking therapy has worked for me very well in the past, and so has reading the wisdom of other people and then trying to put it into practice.

For most of my reading life, I have avidly read personal growth and mind-body-spirit books. I've even bought books that promise to solve problems I don't have – *How To Heal A Toxic Relationship With Your Postman; When Your Pet Rabbit Is A Psychological Vampire* – on the grounds that they might come in handy one day.

Then in 2009, I read a book that changed the way I thought about everything: *The Power of Now* by Eckhart Tolle. Its subtitle is 'A guide to spiritual enlightenment', which I found slightly off-putting until I read it. An alternative subtitle for the general reader might have been 'How to eliminate suffering'.

Although the book contained a lot of what I thought of at the time as 'strange spiritual stuff', it was also an eye-opening and, for me, life-changing analysis of the human tendency to tell ourselves unhelpful stories about other people and incidents in our lives, and to believe untrue things that increase our suffering. Thanks to *The Power of Now*, I was able to opt out of a lot of suffering that I'd have been certain was obligatory and unavoidable in my pre-Eckhart Tolle days.

As well as arguing that suffering is avoidable and unnecessary, Tolle advocates compassion and for-giveness towards others, no matter what they do. One quotation from *The Power of Now* that lodged instantly in my mind is this: 'If her past were your past, her pain your pain, her level of consciousness your level of consciousness, you would think and act exactly as she does. With this realisation comes for-giveness, compassion and peace.'

I mainly agree with Tolle about the benefits of forgiveness, compassion and peace – with one sig-nificant caveat: people can and will always piss us off and do things we think are bang out of order. In order to forgive the *person* more effectively and release the anger and hurt more quickly and com-pletely, we need first to be able to define the *behaviour* as unacceptable. We must be compassionate towards others, yes, but we must honour our own significant negative emotional and psychological experiences by allowing ourselves to hold what I call 'good grudges' that harm no one and simply allow us to remember in a purposeful way instead of acting as if the thing never happened.

In early 2018, a friend recommended to me the Life Coach School podcast, hosted by American life coach Brooke Castillo. I listened to a few episodes and loved everything I heard. Until my introduction to Brooke (I can't call her by her surname – in my head, she and I are good friends, so I'm going to call her Brooke and I know she wouldn't mind) I had never thought about life coaching, apart from when I watched the brilliant episode of *Peep Show* in which Jez becomes a life coach and proceeds to give terrible advice to everyone he knows.

Sometimes, on her podcast, Brooke interviews

other coaches who have their own podcasts. I learned that there are not only general life coaches out there but also many unexpected sub-genres of the profession. I started to explore, and was delighted by the variety that I found in the podcast world. Suddenly a whole new area of self-help had opened up to me. There were weight-loss coaches, relationship coaches, midlife-crisis coaches, coaches for working mothers, coaches who only coach other coaches. My favourite was the decluttering coach who visits your home and, for a sizeable fee, says things like, 'Start with one drawer. Empty it out, only put back the things you want to keep, and throw the rest away.'

My dog walks grew longer and longer as I added more life coaches' and self-help experts' podcasts to my 'must listen' list. As well as Brooke (always and forever my favourite), I started to look forward to new episodes from Kate Swoboda, Robin Sharma, Kara Loewentheil, Tiffany Han, Natalie Lue, Gretchen Rubin and, last but by no means least, Oprah Winfrey and her endless procession of wise and wonderful enlightenment-offering guests. I could and still can spend entire days achieving very little apart from having long-distance help poured into my ears by wise Americans.

This, dear sidekick, is why so many of the books and podcasts I'm choosing to turn to in my attempt to solve the mystery of happiness are by life coaches.

This is why, when I was worried that I was too happy and might benefit from feeling a little less happy with my current life circumstances, I turned to an American life coach called Katherine.

Let me come out of the closet and make a bold claim: I presently believe that the best life coaches are closer to solving the mystery of happiness than any other group of professionals on the planet. And that's why it's crucial to this case that we take witness statements from some of them and hear what they have to say ...

Self Coaching 101 by Brooke Castillo, and the Life Coach School podcast

I knew a lot of Brooke's ideas from listening to her podcast, but it was nevertheless a huge revelation to read this book, that contains a very thorough description and user's guide to her greatest and proudest invention: the CTFAR Model (which stands for Circumstances, Thoughts, Feelings, Actions, Results). The whole 'thoughts create our reality and are responsible for everything' theory that Katherine dazzled me with? That's Brooke's bag, too, as I discovered when I put the rest of my life on hold to spend my every waking hour studying her teachings.

Brooke believes that all circumstances are always neutral – neither positive nor negative. Yes, even a massacre, even the death of a loved one. Brooke's view is that we might deliberately choose and want to feel terrible about both events, and that's fine – and she is at pains to emphasise that she would never wish to feel happy about everything – but her point is that our feelings, and our perceptions of external events and other people's behaviour and character, are *always* caused by our thoughts, and our thoughts are *always* optional; we can change them if we want to.

Brooke encourages us to examine as thoroughly as possible how we're feeling, and then trace that feeling back to a thought. That's step 1.

The next step is to accept that our thought (in response to an always and necessarily neutral circumstance) is what causes our feeling, our feeling then causes our action, and our action brings about our result. Therefore, Brooke argues, the results we see in our lives can always be traced back to our own thoughts. If we accept this premise, we get to take full responsibility for all the results in our lives, and create whatever future results we want using the CTFAR Model.

The only part of the model that we don't have full control over is what Brooke calls the C-line (circumstance), but we can always choose how we want to think about that circumstance, and our thoughts, and never the circumstances, are what create our results. Brooke's self-coaching model is the ultimate in self-empowerment, and I absolutely love it. I think she's the Agatha Christie of her industry: the Queen of Coaching.

She believes that the CTFAR Model can solve any problem, and, at the same time, she encourages us not to expect too much happiness, or only happiness, in our lives. As humans, says Brooke, we are always going to have an emotional balance of feeling great 50 per cent of the time, and 'feeling like ass' the other 50 per cent of the time. Being human involves accepting and welcoming the 50/50. This reminds me of one of the items on my Happiness Hunches longlist, The Positive in the Negative. (I must trim that longlist down to a shortlist … When? I have no time!)

Brooke would say that my having no time is a direct result of thoughts I had in the past. I chose, in the past, to be this busy in my present. My excessive busyness is the Result Line of an old CTFAR Model I was unaware of having created for myself. Even so, it is no one's fault but my own – Brooke would urge me not to beat myself up about this, but rather to choose on purpose what thoughts I want to think to create different results in my future. We must be kind and non-judgemental towards ourselves and others, she says, because only compassion and kindness and good feelings can create lasting positive change.

Okay, so, listen: confession time. One of my weaknesses is that I *love* falling for people and finding new heroes to worship, especially charismatic Americans. And I love even more the idea that there is One Right Answer. (Of course; I'm an Agatha Christie fan.) Having said that, I genuinely believe that Brooke's teachings might be the key to solving all problems, and I cannot disagree with her on any level when she tells me that her CTFAR Model accurately describes and explains absolutely everything.

I know. It's a big claim. But I'm willing to stick my neck out for the CTFAR Model. It's clear, simple, elegant and very hard to disagree with once you understand it properly. (At first, people I've introduced it to tend to say 'What about murdering cute puppies? That's not neutral! That's objectively terrible.' Brooke would say that she too thinks killing cute puppies is terrible, but she's aware that she's choosing to think that and she's happy to stand by that choice and feel sad and angry accordingly whenever she hears of puppies being murdered.)

Her way of looking at the world strongly resembles that of several wise and eminent statue-ish types. Marcus Aurelius said: 'All is as thinking makes it so – and you control your thinking. So remove your judgements whenever you wish and then there is calm – as the sailor rounding the cape finds smooth water and the welcome of a waveless bay.'[1] Shakespeare seems to agree. In *Hamlet*, he wrote, ' ... for there is nothing either good or bad, but thinking makes it so'.[2]

The ancient Stoic Epictetus comprehensively endorsed Brooke's approach to life and self-coaching long before Brooke was born:

> What disturbs men's minds is not events but their judgements on events: for instance, death is nothing dreadful, or else Socrates would have thought it so. No, the only dreadful thing about it is men's judgement that it is dreadful. And so when we are hindered, or disturbed, or distressed, let us never lay the blame on others, but on ourselves, that is, on our own judgements. To accuse others for one's own misfortunes is a sign of want of education; to accuse oneself shows that one's education has begun; to accuse neither oneself nor others shows that one's education is complete.[3]

Interestingly, although Brooke's ideas have so much in common with those of Marcus Aurelius and Epictetus, and though her podcast devotes many episodes to her 'teachers' and to discussions of their ideas, she never mentions the Stoics as being among her influences.

---

1 Marcus Aurelius, *Meditations*
2 *Hamlet*, Act 2, scene 2, lines 253–54
3 *Handbook of Epictetus* (The *Enchiridion*)

The Courage Habit by Kate Swoboda and Your Courageous Life podcast

Kate Swoboda, in her book and her podcast, talks about how to think about and deal with fear, and the importance of establishing new habits if we want to live a more courageous life. By 'more courageous', she means a life that is more in alignment with who we truly are and want to be. She diagnoses a lack of this kind of alignment as one of the major causes of unhappiness, lists some common suboptimal thought patterns and behaviours that trip us up (perfectionism, people pleasing, pessimism and self-sabotage), and suggests practical actions and useful ways to think in tricky situations that can help us to be more in integrity with ourselves.

Like Brooke Castillo, Swoboda is not only a life coach, writer and podcaster, but also the founder of a school that trains life coaches. Unlike Brooke Castillo, Swoboda does not offer a magic-key-to-everything CTFAR Model equivalent. On her podcast, she often says words to the effect that, 'There are no simple answers, there's no magic formula.' Whenever she does, I find myself thinking, simultaneously, 'That's so plausible. How *could* there be a simple answer?' and 'There *is* a simple answer, even if it's not always easy to practise: Brooke's CTFAR Model.'

Unlike Brooke, Swoboda does not appear to

believe that all circumstances are neutral and that only our own thoughts are responsible for causing our feelings; on the podcast in particular, she regularly talks about the behaviour of others from a perspective that assumes that *of course* other people sometimes do objectively awful things that make us feel terrible.

She is also much more overtly political than Brooke. She talks about certain politicians and political situations very negatively, and declares a desire to challenge and resist the force for harm in the world that she believes they represent. Brooke believes in being equally compassionate and uncon- ditionally loving to everyone, no matter what their political perspective or behaviour – because when we negatively judge others, we are in fact harming them and ourselves, and creating suffering. Brooke, like Eckhart Tolle, would undoubtedly say that whenever we cause ourselves upset and disturb our feelings of peace and love for all fellow humans with our strong conviction that someone is terribly harmful, it is our thoughts that are causing the harm and negativity, not the person about whom we're thinking them.

Reading and listening to Kate Swoboda after having immersed myself in Brooke's teachings, I kept finding myself thinking, 'But if you thought about that differently, it wouldn't be the bad thing you've decided it is', though I agree with Swoboda about the importance of focusing on our habits – discarding old ones and creating new ones – if we want to create more happiness, integrity and alignment in our lives. Her approach feels much more a compilation of helpful tips, tools and suggestions around happiness and fulfilment gained through courage rather than a denouement-style, big-reveal 'Here's the answer' or 'Here is my philosophy about how the world works'. She offers plenty of useful clues, though, which I am happy to file away for safekeeping.

The Happiness Project and *The Four Tendencies* by Gretchen Rubin, and the Happier podcast

Rubin is not a life coach. On her website she describes herself as 'a writer who relentlessly explores human nature to understand how we can make our lives better'. Her approach is very much a practical one of experiment followed by result, and it's a personal experiment only; she's telling us about what she did, not what she thinks we ought to do, though she does suggest that we might like to devise and implement happiness projects of our own.

For a year, Rubin chose a different theme to focus on each month – 'Make time for friends'; 'Boost energy'; 'Aim higher' – and then spent the allotted month behaving differently, and consciously, in relation to the month's particular theme. At the end of the year, she was pleased that she had completed her happiness project and she did indeed feel happier. It's not hard to see why: for a year she lived a much more deliberate and curated life instead of one by default. I love her suggestion that we should all design and pursue our own happiness projects, but I miss the magic-answer factor, as I did when I read and listened to Kate Swoboda after first discovering Brooke Castillo.

Gretchen Rubin is the author of another bestselling book, *The Four Tendencies*, which I read immediately after *The Happiness Project*. I bought and read it even though it wasn't on my original list because I knew as soon as I googled Rubin and learned of the book's existence that it would be relevant to the mystery I'm trying to solve. I was right. Ironically, this book proved much more helpful to my happiness investigation than did *The Happiness Project*. In *The Four Tendencies*, Rubin makes an extremely bold claim: that all people, without exception, can be divided into four categories, or tendencies: upholder, obliger, questioner and rebel.

(God, I love bold claims! Is this a problem? Does it mean that I'm more likely to join a weird cult one day? My first instinct is always to be suspicious and sarcastic about everything, so hopefully that will protect me.)

Depending on our 'tendency', Rubin argues that different things make us happy and unhappy. A rebel is in her element when she refuses to meet both outer and inner expectations, but this can make her fail to meet targets others have set for her, as well as ones that she's set for herself – in which case, her 'tendency' might cause her unhappiness long term as she fails to achieve anything. A questioner is only willing to do things he has first questioned and decided make sense. His relentless questioning might give his boss the impression that he's an obstreperous troublemaker, and he might get fired – which might not make him very happy. Upholders strive to meet both outer and inner expectations, but can cause themselves misery with endless 'tightening' of the standards they believe they need to uphold, and so can suffer from stress and burn out, and obligers, who meet outer expectations easily but struggle to fulfil their commitments to themselves, risk feeling unhappy as a result of sacrificing and neglecting their wellbeing as their own values.

Rubin believes that in order to be the happiest we can be and live our best possible lives, we need to take her quiz, find out which is our 'tendency', and then exploit its strengths and take her suggested steps to avoid and address its pitfalls.

Rubin's books are a useful reminder that happiness, and what we need to do in order to achieve it, might be very different for different people. On the other hand …

Unf*ck Your Brain, the podcast – created and hosted by Kara Loewentheil

Another life coach, folks. I hope you will forgive me. What I love about Loewentheil's podcast is her obvious intelligence, and she refers to her listeners as 'my chickens', which I find endearing 98 per cent of the time. (For the other 2 per cent, I think, irritably, 'I'm not a chicken'.) She used to be a lawyer, and a law academic, and she sounds like a proper intellectual. She strikes me as the life coach most likely to do an episode one day about Immanuel Kant's deontological moral theory and how it relates to decluttering our bedside cabinets.

I suspect that Loewentheil would not have much time for Gretchen Rubin's 'Four Tendencies' theory. She believes that it's limiting and unhelpful to think of yourself as any particular type of person, and restrictive, inaccurate and discouraging to view any aspect of your character or behaviour as fixed. She was trained by Brooke Castillo, and is another advocate of the principle that our thoughts create our entire reality – and I'm sure her answer to Rubin would be that any time we want to, we can change our thoughts, feelings and actions, and therefore, by extension, our tendency.

The Pursuit of Happiness by Ruth Whippman (US title *America the Anxious*)

I absolutely loved this book. It's hilarious and scathing, and reading it made me very happy. It contains the phrase 'this llama-shaped tract of human desperation', and is worth reading for that alone. Whippman is a British writer, journalist and film-maker who moved to America and soon became fascinated by the American anxiety-driven obsession with finding happiness. She is deeply suspicious of corporate America's approach to its employees' happiness and of the positive psychology movement, and criticises both from a political perspective, asking if there's something inherently reactionary about the idea that we should rely only on ourselves and our mindful mindset shifts to create our happiness, instead of, for example, life circumstances such as a decent salary, a stable job, good health care and adequate housing.

Whippman argues that governments and employers are absolving themselves of responsibility and avoiding their social justice duties by creating a culture in which citizens and employees are encouraged to believe that they alone are responsible for creating their own happiness. Amusing and chilling in equal measure are the descriptions of corporations that try to convince employees that they can and should be so happy and fulfilled by their work that there's no reason for them ever to want to leave the office.

I'm torn. I can see Whippman's point. 'You go and make yourself happy' does kind of suggest that 'Making you happy is not my job', with perhaps a side order of 'and therefore I can continue to insist that you work nineteen hours a day for £2 an hour'. However … do we really want to entrust our emotional well-being to the very people who are not treating us well in the workplace? I definitely don't. As someone who lived for seven years in one of the scariest and most gun-crime-ridden parts of Manchester, during which time I was regularly mugged, burgled and held up at gunpoint, and was too scared to open my own front door (and yet I was always very happy), I know that sometimes we find ourselves in less than ideal life situations. Yes, it would be lovely if a powerful entity like a government or an employer came and sorted everything out for us, but in reality that very often doesn't happen. And even the poorest, most-mugged-at-gunpoint people who have so little freedom and power, thanks to the socio-economic disadvantages they face, *can* exercise power when it comes to their own thoughts.

Surely that should be emphasised and celebrated? For those who suffer most seriously in the world, the power to choose and use their thoughts to make themselves feel better is often the *only* power they have. I'm therefore inclined to agree more with the people who say, 'Let's teach everyone that it's our own brains that make us happy or sad, not what the rest of the world does', than the ones who say, 'No, let's teach everyone that their unhappiness is someone else's fault and responsibility to solve.'

Of course, none of this means that we can't also take steps to see to it that everyone gets fair wages and great health care. I don't see that positive psychology is at all incompatible with working to make the world a fairer and safer place, though Whippman's descriptions of key popular psychology figures dodging, fudging and evading, like scammers afraid that their con is about to be rumbled, are eye-opening.

*Help Me! One Woman's Quest to Find Out if
Self-Help Really Can Change Your Life*
by Marianne Power

Power is a journalist who was feeling miserable and so decided to work her way through some famous self-help texts, one by one, and practise what they preached in order to test which of the methods was most effective. I was delighted to find that one of her chosen texts was Eckhart Tolle's *The Power of Now*, and my impression (Power doesn't explicitly say so, but it's suggested) is that she found this to be the most life-improving of all the books and approaches she tried. Any friend of Eckhart Tolle is a friend of mine.

How Emotions Are Made by Lisa Feldman Barrett

Barrett is president of the Association for Psychological Science. She's a scientist and an academic, and her thoughts about the making of emotions are laboratory-tested. Her book was a slightly harder slog for a science nincompoop like me – there wasn't even a light-relief chapter about how to declutter my wardrobe – but the slog was entirely worth it because Barrett turns out to be unambiguously in the 'Thoughts Create Feelings' camp (which I think is my camp. I'm starting to feel ready to commit. Almost).

If I was hoping to find some serious scientific muscle with which to back up Brooke Castillo's CTFAR Model, that is exactly what I found in this book. Barrett presents much scientific evidence to demonstrate that our emotions are constructed and do not arise spontaneously in response to circumstances. She gave a TED talk entitled 'You aren't at the mercy of your emotions – your brain creates them.' She also talks a lot about how the culture and society in which we grow up shapes our thoughts and beliefs, and therefore plays a part in creating our feelings. In this respect she is more deterministic than Brooke, who doesn't believe that any of us need to be at the mercy of a set of cultural habits or beliefs unless we choose to be. Brooke emphasises personal and individual responsibility for choosing the thoughts and beliefs we want, no matter what society we grew up in.

Loving What Is by Byron Katie

Byron Katie is a speaker and writer who created something called The Work, which her website describes as a simple, powerful and effective meditation practice. I've also seen it described as a method of enquiry. In this book, Katie argues that human beings cause themselves unnecessary pain by arguing with reality. In her words: 'When you argue with reality, you lose … but only 100 per cent of the time.' Other causes of pain she identifies are: failing to stay in our own business (and instead straying into God's business or other people's business); and believing things that are not true. Although I agree with all of the above, and think that these are incredibly useful concepts to bring to any pursuit of happiness, for an individual or for the world at large, I had a weird experience while reading this book. Katie's work is endorsed by both Eckhart Tolle and Brooke Castillo, and yet in response to almost every paragraph of *Loving What Is*, I found my inner intuitive voice screaming, 'I'm not really sure about this.'

Now, I freely admit that that is: a) a very weird reaction, with nothing whatsoever to back it up; and b) inconsistent of me, because Katie's approach is in many ways very similar to Tolle's and Brooke's. All I can say is that their words, both written and spoken, inspire me and leave me in no doubt that they are significant forces for good on this planet, and Byron Katie's … well, I don't feel the same way about her. I persevered to the end of her book, and concluded that I did not want my solution to the mystery of happiness to involve her personally. When I hear Brooke talking about what Katie believes, it sounds great, and I fully intend to apply some of her sound principles to my life. Yet when I hear Katie herself talk about those principles, I feel much more suspicious of it.

The Work is interesting, however. It has the conceptual clarity and boldness that I am usually drawn to. It involves asking yourself four questions about any thought you have that's causing you distress or disturbing your inner peace:

1. Is it true?

2. Can you absolutely know that it's true?

3. How do you react when you believe that thought?

4. Who would you be without the thought?

Then you're supposed to do 'The Turnaround', where you look at your original thought and see if it's in fact true of you rather than the person you originally had the thought about, or if somehow the exact opposite might be true.

For example, using the thought I've just expressed about Katie's book:

1. Is it true that Loving What Is *is deserving of suspicion?*

No! Of course not. It does not have that innate quality. I'm merely thinking that about it, and plenty of people think otherwise.

2. Can you absolutely know that it's true?

Aren't you listening to my answers? I've just conceded that it is *untrue* as an objective fact. I, however, have that very subjective feeling about it. And I have it very strongly, with no desire to change my thought or feeling.

3. How do you react when you believe that thought?
I decide to use the parts of Katie's theory that I find useful and true, and I puzzle over my emotional response to her book.

4. Who would you be without the thought?
Er … me. A version of myself who trusts my instincts less.

And then the last question: what about The Turnaround?

Um … *I* am deserving of suspicion? Byron Katie's book is the opposite of suspicion-deserving?

I've watched videos in which Katie does The Work with audience members at her events. They start out by saying things like 'My violent partner is ruining my life', then very soon, under Katie's tutelage, they end up saying, 'No, that's not true', and 'I am ruining my own life.'

For me, the big difference between Brooke's approach and Byron Katie's is that Brooke is clear that we *will* sometimes want to choose negative thoughts and feelings, because recognising that something upsetting is nevertheless true for us is important in some instances. And Brooke's emphasis is on helping people to empower themselves and improve their lives, always. When I watch Byron Katie, I can't help thinking, 'Here is a woman trying to convince people that what is true for them in that moment is *not* true for them in that moment. It's almost as if she is doing the very thing she so sensibly advises against: arguing with reality.

The 5 AM Club by Robin Sharma and the Mastery Sessions podcast

Sharma's focus is not so much on happiness as on overall well-being: how to achieve your full potential, become legendary and live a great life. His podcast is one of my favourites. I admire his ambition, his outrageous boldness and his super-high standards in all things (he's very alarmed whenever a member of hotel staff neglects to bring his or her 'A game' to serving the wine or laying down the room service tray). I love all the concepts he's invented and the names he has given them – things like 'The Tight Bubble of Total Focus', 'Rare Air', 'The Leader with No Title', and his 'Four Interior Empires: Mindset, Heartset, Healthset and Soulset'. My favourite of all is his 'Two-Massage Protocol'. This is his idea that in order to be the best versions of ourselves and attain full visionary-hero-legend status, we all need to have two massages per week. I'm in, Robin!

However ... Robin also wants me to get up at 5 a.m. every day, and insists that, above all else, waking up at 5 a.m. is the secret of happiness and success. Robin, I'm afraid I'm out.

You all know by now that I can't help linking everything back to Brooke – and now is no exception. Robin Sharma talks a lot about toxic people and why they are to be avoided. He also believes, and states quite unambiguously and repeatedly, that there are settings and conditions in which we thrive, and ones in which we cannot possibly do so. This directly contradicts Brooke's view that we can thrive in any situation or setting if we choose the right thoughts. In Brooke's philosophy, toxic people do not exist. She advocates feeling unconditional love for everyone and says that we never need remove ourselves from a toxic person's company or a toxic environment, because those things don't exist.

We can, she claims, render any setting or person non-toxic by: a) loving them no matter what they say or do; and b) maintaining our own boundaries in a way that puts us in charge, always, of our own emotional well-being.

I wonder what Katherine and Lyssa would think about this issue of the toxicity or otherwise of other people. I've started to suspect that this might be the one topic about which I disagree with Brooke − which is a shame because, if it weren't for this one thing, I would be significantly closer to solving the mystery of happiness by comprehensively embracing Brooke's way forward.

As it stands, I don't feel I can do so − and it's the 'other people' issue that's blocking me: can we really take full responsibility for our own happiness, irrespective of what other people are doing and how they are treating us?

I'm not sure how to solve this conundrum. Perhaps it's time to attack the mystery from another angle − to revisit my Happiness Hunches Longlist and turn it into a shortlist, with one significant new addition …

6

My Happiness Hunches – the Shortlist

To save you flicking back through the pages of this book (yes, including electronic pages, yes, I know about e-books, thank you), here is my longlist again:

1. Differences Between Things

2. Bad Advice = Good

3. The Cancellation

4. NEAs

5. What if it IS my job?

6. The Positive in the Negative (Grudges)

7. The 65 Days (Eligible? Yes! Why not?)

Dear sidekick, I know you have no idea what any of these happiness clues means. Let me go through them one by one in brief, and then, once I've trimmed them down to a shortlist, I will provide fuller descriptions of the shortlisted items. Does that sound fair? (Say yes.)

1. Differences Between Things. This is my idea, which I think about a lot and still firmly believe in: that most people do not assess the differences between things in an accurate way, and that this failure of assessment leads to all kinds of problems. Happiness and well-being for all would be greatly increased if people thought more accurately about the differences between things.

2. Bad Advice = Good. Easier to guess, perhaps. This is my counter-intuitive theory: that bad advice is good for us because it stimulates our brain into disagreement, which then leads to us giving ourselves the good advice we didn't get originally.

3. The Cancellation. This happiness hunch was inspired by a poem I wrote many years ago – one that remains one of my very favourites of all the poems I've ever written. Here it is:

The Cancellation

On the day of the cancellation
The librarian phoned at two.
My reading at Swillingcote Youth Club
Had regrettably fallen through.

The members of Swillingcote Youth Club
Had just done their GCSEs
And demanded a rave, not poems,
Before they began their degrees.

Since this happened at such short notice
They would still have to pay my fee.
I parked in the nearest lay-by
And let out a loud yippee.

The librarian put the phone down
And muttered, 'Oh, thank the Lord!'
She was fed up of chaperoning
While the touring poet toured.

The girl from the local bookshop
Who'd been told to provide a stall
But who knew that the youth club members
Would buy no books at all

Expressed with a wild gyration
Her joy at a late reprieve,
And Andy, the youth club leader,
And the youth arts worker, Steve,

Both cheered as one does when granted
The gift of eternal life.
Each felt like God's chosen person
As he skipped back home to his wife.

It occurred to me some time later
That such bliss, such immense content
Needn't always be left to fortune,
Could in fact be a planned event.

What ballet or play or reading,
What movie creates a buzz
Or boosts the morale of the nation
As a cancellation does?

No play, is the simple answer.
No film that was ever shown.
I submit that the cancellation
Is an art form all of its own.

To give back to a frantic public
Some hours they were sure they'd lose
Might well be my new vocation.
I anticipate great reviews.

From now on, with verve and gusto,
I'll agree to a month-long tour.
Call now if you'd like to book me
For three hundred pounds or more.

The hunch inspired by this poem is, very simply, that the more often we cancel things, and have things cancelled for us, the happier we are.

4. NEAs. This is my theory that, in order to be truly happy, we need to identify and adhere to at least twenty NEAs, which stands for No Effort Areas. These are exactly what they sound like: areas of life in which we, henceforth, intend to make no effort whatsoever.

5. What if it IS my job? This idea first occurred to me several years ago, and long before I heard, or heard of, Robin Sharma, but it has something in common with his 'leader with no title' theory. It's the idea that, instead of thinking that someone else should take charge of making things better for us or for the world because it's their job or duty to do so, we should treat everything important as if it is our job. No matter what our official role or agreed responsibilities, we can and should make everything our job and responsibility whenever we think we can make a positive difference. (This hunch works well in combination with the NEAs hunch: if we decide that ironing, cleaning out old crisp packets and chocolate-bar wrappers from the car, and remembering the birthdays of people we dislike are NEAs from now on, then we will have more free time to decide that some things are our job that aren't, strictly speaking, our job. Those can then become BEAs or Big Effort Areas.)

6. The Positive in the Negative. This is my theory that sometimes it's good to feel bad, especially … when we're feeling bad! Instead of judging ourselves negatively for the understandable and natural anger or hurt we feel, we can get happier by embracing, welcoming and enjoying our harsher and less peaceful feelings.

7. The 65 Days (Eligible? Yes! Why not?). Hmm. Is The 65 Days eligible? Maybe not. It's not even a theory, so it's low on potential wisdom content. And it's totally made-up. I think I'll leave it out for the time being.

And:

8. Brooke Castillo. This is shorthand for 'Agreeing with Brooke about every single thing and doing everything she advises and recommends'. This is the new item I'm adding to the longlist, to be transferred immediately to the shortlist.

It doesn't take me long to whittle down the options. This is what I'm left with:

The Shortlist

1. The Differences Between Things

2. The Positive in the Negative

3. Brooke Castillo

4. The 65 Days

Okay, now I'm getting somewhere. Would you like to know how I trimmed eight happiness hunches down to four, dear sidekick? First I decided that 'What if it IS your job?' was unnecessary because Item 3, 'Brooke Castillo', kind of covers it. She often talks about how, instead of getting frustrated by what others are not doing, or are doing badly, we should simply take responsibility and action and do it brilliantly ourselves.

Similarly, 'Bad Advice is Good for You', 'The Cancellation' and 'NEAs' can easily be incorporated into 'The Positive in the Negative' – make no effort? Yay! Cancel stuff? Hurrah! Get terrible advice? Winning!

The 65 Days is nagging at the back of my mind and won't go away. It still seems absurd to discuss it, however, because it's not really even a thing. I'll probably take it out later. Or we can all just ignore it. Like the testimony of apparently scatterbrained elderly folk and morose European maids in Agatha Christie novels, it is bound not to be important.

As for Item 1, The Differences Between Things …

Okay, let me tell you a story. I have a dog that I adore. He's a Welsh Terrier and his name is Brewster. I also have many close friends, friendly acquaintances, relatives and work associates who visit my house regularly. Let's say for the sake of argument that there are fifty such people in my life, because that's a nice round number.

All of these fifty people, without exception, have never killed Brewster. However, one of them has repeatedly tried to cause his death, or, at the very least, has tried to *risk* his death, by deliberately leaving the front door open, knowing that he might run out into the street and get run over by a car, or just disappear and never be seen again.

We only got Brewster in January 2014. Before that date, this person – let's call him Charles – never once left my front door open. As soon as Brewster arrived and front door security became vital, Charles suddenly started to leave the front door open regularly.

At first I wondered if he was simply becoming more forgetful, but then an entirely coincidental but highly convenient series of events occurred that provided unquestionable proof, and I was left in no doubt that Charles was taking every opportunity he could to leave my front door wide open in order to endanger my dog and, presumably, to try to create an event that would cause me, my husband and my children immense anguish.

Obviously, I took immediate precautions to ensure Brewster's safety. What does any of this have to do with the differences between things? Well, here's the thing: the difference between someone who has deliberately murdered a loyal and lovely dog and someone who hasn't is immense. Vast. I hope we can all agree on that.

A handful of Charles's and my mutual acquaintances know that Charles has tried to kill Brewster on several occasions. I have shared my proof with them, and, trust me, it's high-qualify proof. It's evidence that would make it impossible for any reasonable person to bring in a verdict of 'Not guilty'.

Some of these mutual acquaintances believe me, some don't, and some say they do but I suspect that, deep down, they don't; they can't bring themselves to believe that someone they're so close to would try to engineer the death of the beloved pet of someone else they're close to. They hate that idea, so they reject it. I totally understand that, and those non-believers are not relevant to our case study.

What's interesting is the behaviour and attitudes of the people who *do* believe it. If Charles had whipped out a gun and shot Brewster dead in front of them, they would have stopped seeing him, stopped inviting him to their homes, stopped thinking of him as a guy they wanted as part of their close circle.

As things stand, they do none of those things, because they think to themselves, 'Come on, there's a huge difference between someone who's murdered a dog and someone who hasn't.' That sounds so true. How could anyone argue with it? In some circumstances it would be true. In this case, it's a negligently inaccurate assessment of the differences between things. Because, my friends, there is *not* a huge difference between someone who's murdered a dog and someone who hasn't when the person who hasn't is someone who has repeatedly tried to do that very thing.

As I've told so many writers over the years, and will tell many more once Dream Author, my coaching programme for writers, gets underway: the difference between J. K. Rowling and a writer who has only so far written one much-rejected manuscript is not necessarily as massive as it at first seems. If the unpublished writer is absolutely determined to pursue her writing dreams no matter what, and will never, ever stop believing she can succeed, and takes action accordingly, then she is far more similar to J. K. Rowling than she is to another unpublished writer who isn't sure if the effort and pain are worth it and is considering giving up on her writing dream.

Being able to measure and perceive, clearly, the differences between things is crucial if we want to increase our happiness and well-being. Also …

Does Brooke Castillo (who has two dogs that she adores, Rory and Rocket) honestly, seriously and for real think that I should unconditionally love someone who has tried to murder my dog?

Damn. I think the answer to that is yes. Villain compassion and all that. Other people's actions are never the cause of our unhappiness. Even if they kill our dogs.

Really?

I have a problem here: a clash of shortlisted hunches. Brooke Castillo is clashing with The Differences Between Things. I definitely don't think I'd be happier if I loved Charles the would-be dog-killer unconditionally – not unless I made myself considerably more foolish and reckless at the same time, and I don't want to do that. I want to be able to treat people differently, and feel differently about them, based on their actions and what kind of people I think they are.

And yet when I think about Charles, I am not filled with warm, loving feelings. Does that mean that I'm less happy than I might be, and should try to change my thoughts?

I can't solve this one alone. If you have an opinion about this, dear sidekick, please feel free to share it with me. To help us both reach a conclusion, I'm going to bring back the experts, because until we understand how our relationships with others affect our happiness, the mystery cannot be declared solved, or anywhere near solved.

7

Talking to Life Coaches about Other People

I'm keeping a secret from both Katherine and Lyssa. Neither of them knows that I've written a self-help book called *How to Hold a Grudge* or that I have a podcast on the theme of why holding grudges is good for us if we do it in the right way, also called How to Hold a Grudge. I've recently recorded Season 3. I forgot to mention that when I was describing my work commitments to Lyssa and Katherine. I think I was embarrassed to admit quite how many work projects I had taken on, in case they thought I was beyond bonkers.

In my second sessions with both coaches, I will not be discussing or even mentioning my workload. I've actually not been thinking much about it at all recently, because I've been so busy focusing on trying to solve my happiness mystery. As Brooke says, our thoughts determine our entire life experience, so if you never think about something – I mean, like, *never* – then for you it is as if that thing doesn't exist. That's the approach I'm adopting at the moment in relation to everything but this investigation. It's working brilliantly. (Just don't tell Poirot – I don't think he's noticed yet.)

It's probably because of all the work I've done as the world's only Grudge Guru (this is a true and official title, I swear) that I'm so keen to talk to Katherine and Lyssa about the always problematic issue of Other People. I want to see if they agree more with Brooke, who believes that everyone is innately lovable, or with Robin Sharma, who believes that some people are toxic and are to be avoided.

Instead of recounting the traumatic story of Charles and Brewster, which is a years-old and solved problem, I decide to pick my two currently-most-aggravating Other People dilemmas to discuss with Katherine and Lyssa. They can get stuck into one interpersonal conundrum each, and, if I'm lucky, I'll end up with both neatly solved for the bargain price of approximately $300.

I've also resolved not to tell either of them that I'm trying to settle a debate between me and my two imaginary friends, Brooke and Robin. Not everyone needs to have a full overview at all times – and if that's not one of the commonly accepted tenets of happiness, then it certainly should be.

Dilemma 1 (Katherine) – The Weird Ego

K: So, how's your work situation since we last spoke?

Me: Actually, I want to talk about something different today, if that's okay. Though …

K: What?

Me: It's about a friend. Well, an ex-friend. I mean … officially we haven't fallen out, but I no longer think of her as a proper friend.

K: Why not?

Me: I need to be totally honest about this, even if it makes me sound horrible and mean.

K: Do *you* think you're being horrible and mean to this person?

Me: Definitely not outwardly. But in my head, I think I might be. But then, whenever I think that, another part of me thinks, 'No, I'm not. I do not have to like everybody. That can't be a moral requirement.'

K: Tell me about your friend.

Me: I used to really enjoy seeing her and talking to her and then I just … stopped. I still care about her and want the best for her, but … The thing is, she's still a good person, as good as she ever was, but I don't think I *like* her any more. I've gone off her.

K: At a certain point, your thoughts about her changed?

Me: Yes. I started to notice something about her that I hadn't noticed so much before. I don't know if she became more insufferable or if I became less tolerant, but we spent a weekend together and after it, I thought, 'That's it. I don't want to spend any more time with her.'

K: And do you understand why you thought that?

Me: Yes. This is the part where I'm going to sound horrible. She's got a very weird and demanding ego. It's not that she only cares about herself and no one else – she's actually very kind and caring and selfless in some ways. But … ugh, it's hard to explain. It's like her ego is constantly bothering her and leaping up and demanding attention. And so for anyone who's with her, it's a bit like being with someone who always has a very demanding dog in tow. You're trying to talk to them and have a nice day together, but they're constantly being distracted by the endless demands of this high-maintenance poodle. And then you have to notice and respond to the poodle too, and the poodle just takes over everything. Not that I've got anything against poodles, I love poodles. I love all dogs. But it's like her ego pops up and whispers to her 'Make me feel better, quick!' and then she does this thing – almost pathologically – where she makes everything about her. Every conversation, wherever it starts, ends up with her saying in dozens of different ways how brilliant she is, and woe betide anyone who doesn't instantly realise that. And I end up, whenever I have any dealings with her, feeling as if I'm being sold a lie: what's supposed to be a friendship feels like me endlessly servicing, accommodating and cringing at her weird ego. And occasionally being ticked off by it!

K: Ticked off?

Me: Told off. Chastised. Once or twice she's directly criticised me in a ridiculously smug way for things I've done that are *nowhere near as bad* as the worst thing she's done. Not that it's a contest – I know this. But I would never dream of saying to her, 'Please can you stop wiping your weird ego all over the place whenever we're together?' or 'Please can you stop drinking way too much and massively embarrassing me in public?' She does that too. She doesn't mean to do any of it, like, *at all*. I think it might be a kind of deep insecurity, which has led to a constant need to prove and validate herself, and to make everything about her and her needs and her agenda. I get why she's like she is – her parents divorced quite horribly and dramatically when she was little.

K: Sophie, there's so much judgement in everything you've just said. Of your friend, but also of yourself: when you said how horrible and mean you were going to sound.

Me: Yes. This is what I want to talk about. I quite like having a brain that I use to make judgements about my own behaviour and other people's. Like, I suspect this is a huge asset to me!

This is, in fact, what my self-help book *How to Hold a Grudge* is all about. It would be odd if I mentioned it now, so I keep quiet about it.

Me: And so, because I've always found this aspect of my thinking to be helpful to me, I'm wondering if it might be totally fine to just … go ahead and make some judgements? While totally accepting that I'm a fallible human who might be wrong, obviously.

K: How do you feel when you judge yourself as horrible and your friend as insufferable and embarrassing, and compare her ego to a demanding poodle?

Me: Um … fine? And I'm not saying I think it's necessarily horrible of me to be thinking this way about her. That's what I want to know: is it? I feel sorry for her, I don't think she's a bad person *in any way* – she is, without doubt, a force for good in the world. However, I'm also aware that … I don't like her much any more. And … is that okay?

K: How do you feel when you think the thought, 'I don't like her much any more'?

Me: One third absolutely fine, one third guilty, one third intellectually curious – keen to solve the mystery of whether I'm the problem or she's the problem. Have you heard of a life coach called Brooke Castillo?

K: Oh yes. She's actually my hero.

Me: I agree. She believes that there's no such thing as a toxic person – that the other person's behaviour is never the problem. The problem is always our thoughts about that person, and we can always choose to cause ourselves less suffering and bring more love into our lives by thinking about people differently: by accepting them for who they are, and deciding they're fine exactly as they are. And then we can love them no matter what they say or do to us, and we benefit from that love because, by feeling it, we're bringing more love-experience into our lives. That all sounds great on one level.

K: Only on one level?

Me: Yes. On several other levels, it sounds weird and wrong. And other life coaches disagree: Robin Sharma talks a lot about the importance of avoiding toxic people and eliminating them from our lives. And Kate Swoboda, who also goes by the name 'Kate Courageous', did a podcast episode recently about how damaging it is to describe someone as 'toxic', but it was clear from the episode as a whole that she *totally* believed that the person who'd called *her* toxic was pretty toxic, even if she was expressing that in enlightened life-coach language.

K: How would you feel if, instead of thinking that you don't like your friend any more, you were to think, 'I love my friend, no matter what, no matter how she behaves'?

Me: I'd feel worse. The thought that I have to like people equally irrespective of their behaviour—

K: Why equally? I didn't say equally. We all prefer some people to others. And loving someone doesn't mean you have to spend time with them. It can simply mean that you wish them well and don't judge them for who and what they are. You stop defining their behaviour as wrong in some way.

Me: If you're talking about a more general kind of 'I hope she's okay and I want the best for her', then absolutely, I agree. But for me, that's compatible with forming the judgement that I don't enjoy spending time with her.

K: Why is that? Why don't you like—

Me: I've just told you. Demanding poodle ego taking over everything all the time.

K: That's the part that we need to look at. You think the reason you don't like her is because of *her*.

Me: Oh, I get it. It's because of my thoughts, you're going to say.

K: Yes.

Me: Same as with my busy work schedule?

K: It's the same in every area of our lives. And once we realise this, we have complete freedom to create whatever kind of mental and emotional experience we want. This is what I don't think you understand yet on a deep level.

Me: Right. So, if I change my *thoughts* about her, I can like her as much as I ever did, without her changing her behaviour at all.

K: Exactly.

Me: But what if I don't want to change my thoughts? What if I want to like people who *don't* make me feel irritated and slightly used for ego-building purposes *more*, and people who do, less?

K: So you think your friend makes you feel irritated and used? It's her behaviour that's making you feel that way?

Me: (*sighs*) You think my *thoughts* about her make me feel irritated and used?

K: I know that it's your thoughts. That's how the world works.

Me: Yes. Right.

K: And it's great news!

Me: It is?

K: Yes, because it gives you back all your power. She's not making you feel any way at all. She's just being her, and she has no power over what goes on in your brain. *You* have all the power to decide what you want to believe and how you want to feel. And I guess my question to you is: why would you choose to think, 'I don't like her', and feel less affection, when you could think, 'I love her, no matter what', and feel the benefit of that love in *your* life? *We* are the ones who experience the love or lack of it that we're feeling when we think about others. Can you see that? Can you see that it would benefit you to love her no matter what, without judgement?

Me: Yes and no. Yes for all the obvious reasons that you've been saying, and that Brooke says, but also no because … I don't *want* to like amazing people and annoying people equally. I want to prefer better things to worse things – and that goes for people too.

K: Do you think there are better and worse people?

Me: Not innately, in terms of ... I don't know, their soul's potential ...

(This is what happens when you spend too much time chatting to American life coaches, folks. Be warned.)

Me: ... but in terms of behaviour, and enjoyableness to be around? Yes, I do. Having judgement and using it to improve my life experience and the world if possible ... ultimately, that makes me happier than adopting an equal-love-for-everyone-and-no-judgement approach would.

K: Yet you feel guilty about your current feelings towards your friend.

Me: Maybe. I can't decide if I should or if it's totally fair enough. The thing is, I borderline worship Brooke Castillo, and agree with 99 per cent of what she says. So the few snippets I'm inclined to disagree about probably bother me more than they should.

K: You use the word 'should' a lot.

Me: Is that bad? Should I stop? Oops.

K: Ha!

Me: Also, Brooke says that when we judge other people's behaviour as negative, we're the only ones who feel the effects of our own negativity, but … that's not true. I know from my own experience that it's not. For example, I once behaved in a cowardly way, and people judged my behaviour negatively and I lost a friend over it – and it was useful to me to feel the impact of that, and to have that consequence: losing the friend, having people obviously think worse of me. It all helped me to realise that my cowardice was wrong, and was causing me more problems than it was solving. I addressed it, and … I'm not a coward any more. And in other situations, people think I've done things wrong and I'm certain I haven't, and that *they're* wrong. I mean … the ability to judge is useful. That's why it's better to be a human being than a … I don't know, a goldfish. Brooke often says that we're lucky to be the only animals with a prefrontal cortex or higher brain – and part of what that brain can do is form judgements, create value systems and decide that it doesn't like certain things.

K: We can always use our brain in whatever way we choose to – that's our privilege.

Me: Exactly. And … there is such a thing as objective truth, right?

K: I still think it's worth asking yourself why you'd rather think 'I don't like my friend any more' than think 'I love my friend, no matter what'. Which thought would make you feel better? Which would bring more love into your life?

Me: I mean … but, like, Eva Braun could have adopted that approach when she was choosing between the thoughts 'I love Hitler no matter what' and 'I'm starting to worry that Hitler's not so great and maybe I should steer clear.' Even if you want to leave moral judgement out of it and think only about what's going to make Eva feel good, the first thought led to her ending up dead in a bunker. The second would almost certainly have given her a longer, happier life.

K: Your friend is not Adolf Hitler, though, is she?

Me: No, of course not. I'm just trying to establish some basic kind of ... logical guidelines. Look, let's say I *do* feel guilty about not liking my friend any more: maybe that's fine. I don't want to like her as much as I did or hang out with her, given her behaviour, but also I feel a bit guilty about that from time to time. Isn't that just human? I mean, the world isn't perfect.

K: Isn't it? What if it is? Is it possible that the world and your friend are perfect just as they are?

Me: Oh, my God.

Dilemma 2 (Lyssa) – The Uninterested Friend

For Lyssa, I choose a different dilemma – another one involving a friend. This friend loves me to bits and would drop everything to help me if I were critically ill or dying. When I'm healthy and basically okay, however, she shows no interest in me or my life. Like, zero interest. Not even a glimmer of curiosity once a year. I can and regularly do ask her question after question about her life and the lives of her husband, daughters and dogs, and she'll answer (though not in much detail), but she never reciprocates.

It's very weird. Another mystery, in fact. Maybe

she's just not much of a talker and is happy to be more self-contained.

Once, when I received a horrible email while at her house and burst into tears, she responded by standing up and saying, 'I'm off to bed'. Another time she was at my house watching TV and someone exciting who I was about to start working with appeared on the screen. 'Oh!' I said. 'Look, it's X! That's who I'm working with on Y.' My friend acted as if I hadn't said a word. She didn't even glance at the screen. She pulled her phone out of her bag and started scrolling through her Facebook notifications. In my opinion, that's not how a good friend ever behaves.

Are these only my thoughts, though, or are they facts? Could it be my beliefs about her that are causing my frustration, rather than her lack of interest in me? Could I solve the problem and feel great about her immediately by thinking, 'She never asks questions or shows any curiosity about my life, what I think or how I feel, and that's totally fine'?

This might seem like a strange topic to be spending so much time on, dear sidekick, but it feels important to get to the bottom of whether or not other people can or cannot make us happy or unhappy. I hope you can see why. Anthony Seldon, author of *Beyond Happiness*, certainly believes that they can. So does Robin Sharma. Eckhart Tolle and Byron Katie disagree: they're more in the Brooke

Castillo camp, and think that it's only the stories we tell ourselves and then believe that make us unhappy. I need to know who's right before I can move on in my investigation.

Lyssa has an interesting take on the situation. My first question to her is: how can you love and care about someone and show zero interest in them? Is that possible? I've told my friend about fourteen times, for example, that I'm planning to launch a coaching programme for writers called Dream Author. Every time, since the very first time, she's said, 'I know'. Not once has she asked what it's going to involve, or any questions about it at all.

L: You seem certain she loves and cares about you in spite of her disinterested behaviour. Is that definitely true?

Me: Uninterested.

L: Huh?

Me: Never mind. Sorry, go on.

L: Maybe she doesn't care at all.

Me: No, she definitely does. Whenever she's in a terrible state, I'm the first person she comes to and wants to talk to.

L: That might mean she thinks you can help her in those circumstances.

Me: I do help her.

L: Right, but that help is for her. That's her taking from you, for her own benefit. She could do that for her own sake, without caring about you at all, couldn't she?

Me: Oh, I see. Yes, but … Yes. I suppose so.

L: I'm not saying she doesn't love you. She may well. Different people love in different ways.

Me: She would be a wreck if I died. I know she would. She's just not interested in me while I'm alive – which makes no sense to me. Like, I *know* that if I died, if she didn't have me any more, she'd be properly devastated. Yet … here I am, and we meet regularly, and she never even asks me how I am or what I've been doing lately. Actually, to be fair … maybe one time out of five she will ask me one question. But then, if I start to answer properly, her eyes wander and she starts kind of going, 'Yeah, yeah', in a clipped, distracted way, and it's clear she's not really listening. She quite often looks away or walks away when I'm in mid-sentence. So then I think, 'Why bother even trying to talk to her?' and, next time she asks me a rare question, I answer in three words or less, and she never asks a follow-up question. I mean, she never seems to *actually want to know* what's going on in my mind or life. I would wonder if she secretly resents me, but we have a mutual friend who says she shows the same complete lack of interest in her stuff.

L: I think it's so interesting that you're obsessing about what her behaviour means as if it's a mystery you want to solve.

Me: It is! And also … there are lots of people whose lack of interest I genuinely wouldn't give two hoots about, but … from her, it actually makes me sad. I feel as if … This is going to sound melodramatic and I know it's not true, but I feel as if she's cut me off, even though I see her regularly. When I'm in her company, I feel as if my existence is being negated. Like, cancelled out.

L: There's an obvious way to try to solve the mystery: talk to her about it.

Me: Er, no way.

L: Why?

Me: Isn't it obvious?

L: Not to me.

Me: Oh.

L: You could work on solving a different mystery: why do you keep doing this to yourself?

Me: With my thoughts, you mean? I could definitely work on feeling not negated when she's around, that's true.

L: You could. But what I meant is that you could choose not to see her any more.

Me: That would be more painful than the current situation. I don't want to lose her from my life, even though I don't feel she's properly with me even when she's with me. There's a strong sentimental and symbolic attachment, though, and I don't want to break it. I love her, I guess, even with the total lack of interest factored in.

L: Why don't you want to talk to her about it?

Me: It wouldn't make me feel better. She'd give some reason or excuse, and she'd insist she does care and is interested in me, and then she'd make sure to ask, like, six pre-arranged questions every time she saw me from then on—

L: Sophie, you don't know what she'd say or do.

Me: True. Not the specifics, but … I *do* know that whenever I've been angry or upset with anyone and talked to them about it, I never ended up feeling better. Like, not even once in 48 years.

L: Wow.

Me: I know, right? As Jerry Seinfeld said: 'People. They're the worst.' That's a joke! I think people are great. Well, some of them. But … whenever I've gone from feeling terrible to feeling better, it's always been *me* that's made me feel better by … making a new decision or resolution or something.

L: That's actually always true, for all of us. Our thoughts create our reality.

Me: So you agree with Katherine and Brooke. Have you heard of Brooke Castillo?

L: Everyone's heard of Brooke! She's the highest-paid female life coach in the world, I think.

Me: Brooke would say that when I feel sad about my friend who shows no interest in me, it's *only* my thoughts that are causing my sadness, and not in any way my friend's behaviour. Do you think that's true?

L: If I answer yes, you'll misunderstand me.

Me: What do you mean?

L: Well … your thoughts are what cause your choices, right? You choose what to do based on what you're thinking.

Me: Yes.

L: It seems to me that you keep making choices in relation to this friend that guarantee the continuation of your suffering.

Me: Huh!

L: You won't talk to her about it and you continue to see her, *and* you tell yourself over and over that she's injuring you on a psychic level. How will your pain ever end, then?

Me: Maybe it won't. If it doesn't … you're saying that's my fault?

L: It's never helpful to look at relationships in terms of fault.

Me: All right, not fault, then. My doing? I'm causing my own pain?

L: Somewhere deep down, do you think there might be a thought you're having – maybe one you're not conscious of – that begins with the words, 'I want to carry on suffering because …'?

Me: No. Honestly, I don't.

L: Humour me. If there *was* that thought somewhere in your subconscious brain, how might that sentence end? 'I want to carry on suffering in this friendship because …'

Me: Erm … to prove myself right that people are endlessly disappointing?

L: Yes! That sounds true to me.

Me: You agree? I thought you were going to argue with me. People are just *so* disappointing, aren't they?

L: That's not what I meant, Sophie. I meant that I agree that you're probably wanting your theory to be proved right, your belief that people are endlessly disappointing. It always feels comforting to have our long-held beliefs proved right.

Me: Wait a minute. You said 'if'. *If* my subconscious mind contained a sentence that began 'I want to carry on suffering in this friendship because …', how would that sentence end. I was answering conditionally. And creatively. That isn't my actual subconscious thought.

L: Are you sure?

Me: Yes. I have many conscious thoughts: I love my friend, I don't think she treats me very well, and I'm sad about that. I also don't want to lose her, crap though she might be. Those are my thoughts. And …

L: And what?

Me: I've trapped myself in a suffering situation, and I keep insisting that all the possible ways out it are impossible and can't be considered. Just like with my work situation.

L: Yes. Precisely. And you know what?

Me: What?

L: That's enough. Understanding that that's what's going on for you is enough.

Me: No, it's not.

It really isn't. Not if I want to solve the mystery of happiness.

Is it possible that I do want to carry on suffering so that I can continue to believe that people are disappointing? No, I don't think so – genuinely. What's more likely is that I don't trust anyone but myself to make me feel better, so when I'm feeling sad or angry or suboptimal in any way, the only person I ever want to talk to about it is myself. Or paid experts, like Katherine and Lyssa – professional solvers of people's individual happiness mysteries who aren't part of my real life.

I don't want people I know to know too much about what I'm thinking or feeling if my emotional state contains any element of sadness or anger. If I'm feeling great and thinking cheering, jolly thoughts, that's something I'm always happy to share with everyone, from close friends and relatives to the postman and my dental hygienist.

Weird. Maybe I need to talk to a psychotherapist instead of a life coach – someone with a framed photo of Freud or Jung on their wall instead of a framed motivational motto.

Later that evening I listen to an interview with Brooke Castillo on someone else's podcast, in which Brooke says (unaware that a happiness detective is monitoring her every word) that the things she teaches now about how to thrive and live your best and happiest possible life are the direct opposite of everything she learned when she studied psychology at university. This makes me think again about 'proper' therapy.

Wait … didn't Brooke also do a podcast episode about the differences between therapy and coaching? Or did I imagine that?

What if all the therapists think all the coaches are wrong?

If I'm being fair, I must admit that therapy changed my life hugely for the better long before coaching did. For a few months in 2011, I had several psycho-analytic hypnotherapy sessions with a lovely woman called Juliet. In our first few sessions, I talked a lot about a man who had behaved for many years in a way that had terrified and oppressed me. I kept stressing, however, that he had not meant to do so; he was genuinely doing his best in life, including in the way he treated me. He wasn't very psychologically strong, and simply wasn't capable of better behaviour.

Juliet always seemed rather cross with him on my behalf, which I appreciated. Then one day I was feeling unusually raw as a result of the therapy, and less inclined than usual to being understanding about everything. I said, 'You know what? He actually persecuted me for about fifteen years.' Juliet raised both her hands in the air and shouted, 'Yes! Hooray! Finally, you can see it!'

Juliet definitely didn't think that it was only my thoughts that had persecuted me for all those years.

Suddenly, I am desperate to talk to my friend Helen, who's an existential psychotherapist. Helen is a regular guest on my How to Hold a Grudge podcast and she contributed significantly to the book too. She has told me many times that she could never be my therapist because we're friends, but we can and do discuss psychological matters, often involving grudges, regularly.

I need to talk to her. Why didn't I think of it sooner? It seems to me that Helen could be a key witness in this investigation. I remember her, in a previous conversation we had, saying that human interactions are relational. Does that mean that she believes we cannot be happy if, for example, our nearest and dearest are secretly plotting to kill our dog?

It's time to find out ...

8

A Conversation with an Existential Psychotherapist

Helen and I have some new episodes of the How to Hold a Grudge podcast to record for Season 3, which is starting in November. What better setting in which to grill her about the thorny issue of We Make Ourselves Happy versus Other People Make Us Happy?

Episode 9 of Season 3 is called 'Against My Better Grudgement'. This is the blurb I drafted for it, long before I set myself the task of solving the happiness mystery:

Being judgemental is bad, we tend to think, but using our judgement is essential. So how do we distinguish between good judging and bad judging? Having a lower opinion of some people than others has to be okay, surely, even if one's aim and wish is to be all-forgiving and grudge-free. Sophie and Helen discuss the ways in which our own ethics and opinions in relation to infidelity and meat-eating, among other things, can influence how lenient/empathetic we're able to be where those issues are involved.

Over dinner, once we've finished recording, Helen reminds me that we discussed the matter of whether we're solely responsible for our own feelings of happiness or unhappiness in Season 1 of the podcast. She is as unequivocal on this issue now as she was then.

Helen: I don't agree with anyone who says that our thoughts are solely responsible for creating our feelings. Human beings are social animals. We have relationships with other humans, and the way they treat us is obviously going to affect us emotionally. And sometimes people treat us badly – they just do. And when they do, it can harm our psychological recovery to believe that it was our own thoughts, rather than them, that harmed us.

Me: Though we probably would suffer less, overall, if we loved everyone in the world no matter what, and decided that whatever anyone did was totally fine.

Helen: But it isn't.

Me: I agree. I don't think it is either. Some things people do make me unhappy, and I *don't* like some people as much as others – and Brooke does say that we might sometimes choose to feel sad or angry. The important thing, she says, is to realise that only our thoughts, and never the words or actions of others, create our feelings. I think that's probably completely true. I'm choosing to think some things are grudge-worthy, and I like my choice and its results, but … it *is* a choice based on my thoughts.

Helen: I don't think it's true that we can always choose what to think – though obviously we can work on changing our thoughts. But in the moment, especially if someone treats us shockingly badly, we have spontaneous thoughts and feelings that arise in response to what others do and say to us. And we always will! And … should we necessarily try to brainwash ourselves out of our original thoughts?

Me: No, not if we don't want to. And if we don't want to, then that's our thought, isn't it? It's our voluntary, deliberate thought – which is fine.

Helen: But Brooke seems to want to claim that it's all within our power, and it isn't. We are transactional beings, and we *are* affected by other people. It's not all about us and always within our control to create our experience. Some thoughts we can't change, no matter how much inner work we do – and then we might end up feeling like our suffering really is our fault. The American life-coach approach feels much too close to gaslighting. Imagine if someone has been really cruelly treated by someone else and then a life coach tells them that the person who's been awful to them hasn't caused their suffering – that only their own thoughts have caused their suffering. It absolves the truly blameworthy person of responsibility, and makes the victim feel that she's causing her own pain.

Me: Katherine and Brooke, and possibly Lyssa too, think it's empowering to realise that you have the freedom and power to think whatever you want – whatever's going to benefit you most – about everything that happens in your life. I agree with that. If it matters to you to think, 'He treated me appallingly' and you have a good reason for thinking it, Brooke wouldn't tell you to change your thought. She just wants everyone to be aware that they have 100 per cent of the power to decide how they want to feel about everything from now on, and to choose the thoughts that are going to create those feelings.

Helen: But, like I said, we can't always change our thoughts and feelings. It's too easy for Katherine's approach, or Brooke's, to be used by people who've treated others terribly to let themselves off the hook. 'It's not my fault you feel awful. Yes, I did say you were a worthless waste of space, but it's not my words that hurt you. It's the *thoughts* you had about my words.' It's a kind of victim-blaming.

Me: I see what you mean, but I don't think it is. It's not intended that way. It's basically saying to people, 'Whatever has happened and whatever others are doing, you don't have to think of yourself as a helpless victim, and it's always better for you if you don't. You'll be better off if instead you think, 'This is what I want to believe about this situation, and here's why, and no one but me can control how I feel.' I'm definitely 'all in', as Brooke would say, up to that point. The part I struggle with is the unconditional-love-for-all-and-never-judging-others-makes-us-happier bit. When I told Katherine that I *wanted* to like my weird-ego friend less, she definitely thought that wasn't ideal.

As I'm saying all this to Helen, I find myself thinking that there are problems with both of the extreme positions:

Extreme 1: accepting that other people's terrible behaviour is the cause of our unhappiness.

Extreme 2: never judging anyone, unconditionally loving everyone, and believing that no behaviour is objectively unhappiness-creating because all circumstances (including other people's actions and words) are inherently neutral until we have a thought about them.

I am confident that neither of these is the solution to the mystery of happiness – at least, not without caveats. The first is too disempowering. The second seems to ignore some basic facts about human nature.

Helen: It's interesting that you never want to talk to anyone about it when they've upset you, though. I'm the opposite. If a good friend or someone I care about hurts me or makes me angry, I usually tell them how I'm feeling, and I'd want them to tell me. How else can you sort it out?

Me: I know. It *is* interesting. I think as a child I learned a lesson that … maybe isn't true? But it's very difficult to unlearn it now.

Helen: What lesson?

Me: That life is vastly easier and I suffer much less if I pretend to be totally fine with other people behaving in ways that I dislike and disapprove of, or that cause me pain. Like, as a child and young adult, if I'd said, 'I think you're behaving like a tyrannical, emotionally manipulative bully', to people who had power over me, I'd definitely have suffered more.

Helen: Yes – and, as you say, those patterns are formed so early in our lives.

Me: Also … if the form the emotional tyranny takes is endlessly getting yelled and bellowed and sulked at for everything you're supposedly doing wrong in every aspect of your life, and having affection and approval totally withdrawn whenever you disappoint someone just by being who you are, aren't you more likely to turn into an adult who instinctively feels that to even hint towards a criticism of someone else's behaviour, ever, would be a form of you bullying them?

Helen: Yes, definitely. This is somewhere where you probably could change your instinctive thoughts if you wanted to, though it might be hard. You could think, like me, that if you care about a relationship being as good and close as it can be, then you can sometimes explain to someone how you feel about something they said or did. You can do that without yelling or sulking or withholding affection. They might welcome the chance to explain what they meant.

Me: I know. You're right. But it feels to me so controlling — and such bad manners too — to tell someone that something they did made you feel bad. I can't imagine that ever feeling like anything apart from 'Please dance to my tune and behave in ways I prefer in future'. But then I know from listening to Brooke's podcast that withholding my true feelings about the person or the situation is just a different kind of controlling behaviour — one in which I retain all the control because they don't know there's a situation and so can't respond to what's truly going on.

Helen: Yeah, which is less honest. I prefer to be as honest as possible.

Me: God, I don't. Not about my feelings. But maybe I should try it just once – total honesty, with either the weird-ego friend or the totally uninterested friend.

One of Brooke Castillo's favourite sayings pops into my mind: if you don't know what to do, just do something.

She's right. What if I've been going about this the wrong way, trying to find a theory that works for me 100 per cent? What if searching for the solution to the mystery of happiness isn't about working out a perfect theory? What if, instead, it's about *doing* more rather than thinking and philosophising?

I know what this means. Or at least, I know what I'm choosing to think it means.

It's time for the 65 Days.

9

The 65 Days

The 65 Days is an idea I had a few years ago, while planning an ambitious crime novel that I have wanted to write for some time. (And I will, though I haven't yet – it's on my 'To do later, when less busy' list. This list is the only one I've ever made that has a subtitle: 'Definition of less busy: a family member approaching with a mild-mannered "Can I ask you a favour?" no longer makes my heart pound as I consider pretending not to recognise them and/or answering in pretend Portuguese.)

The 65 Days is the tentative and provisional title of a self-help book that the main character of my yet-to-be-written crime novel has published. It has made her famous, in fact. And – here's my thinking; you can let me know if the logic holds up – even though it doesn't exist apart from in my mind, it might still be useful to this investigation of happiness. I have tried, as you've witnessed, to ignore it, because it seemed rather silly to include it, but it keeps popping up in my mind, so let's give it a go.

Unlike so many other possible solutions to the mystery of happiness that we've looked at so far, it is not a theory. It contains no element of theory, in fact. And I don't know about you, but I need a break from wondering, 'But is that true? What if it's not? And how the hell can we ever know?'

I'm tired of theories, dear sidekick. It's time for some action. What if this mystery cannot be solved by theories alone? I feel as if that might be — and indeed *should* be — the case.

So ... am I too proud to go to a made-up self-help book for help? No, I am not.

The 65 Days is a simple experiment that enhances the life of anyone who undertakes it, hence the huge global success of my not-yet-created protagonist's slim volume. The experiment involves starting at the beginning of a year (not necessarily a calendar year — any year will do) and dividing that year into 300 'regular' days and 65 'special purpose' days. You then fulfil the special purpose that is prescribed on the 65 days, do whatever you'd normally do or whatever you want to do on the other 300 days, and monitor the effects this has on your feelings throughout the year. (Spoiler: the effects are extraordinary and life-changing for everyone who 'does' the 65 Days.)

After much searching on my old computer, I managed to find a list of the 65 'special purpose' days that I jotted down when I first had the idea. My not-yet-created heroine is very prescriptive and has no intention of leaving it up to every reader of the book to choose 65 special purposes for him – or herself.

Why 65? Well, because in the novel I haven't yet written, the heroine has a sinister so-called philanthropist father who forces her and her sister (using emotional blackmail) to live punitively selfless lives. He suggests (in a way they can't refuse) that they should spend 300 days of each year thinking only of other people, and spend only 65 days thinking about themselves, having fun, and doing what they want to do; that is the proportional division of their time that he has decided is moral, so it becomes a family rule.

My fictional heroine later reclaims the idea of the 65 Days, and turns something that was used to torment her as a child into something that can help her and be a force for good in her life as an adult.

Here is the list of the 65 Special Purpose Days:

Day 1 – Promise Something

Day 2 – Admit Something

Day 3 – Invent Something

Day 4 – Test Something

Day 5 – Buy Something

Day 6 – Invite Someone

Day 7 – Write to Someone

Day 8 – Laugh at Something

Day 9 – Make Something

Day 10 – Remove Something

Day 11 – Plan Something

Day 12 – Cancel Something

Day 13 – Add Something

Day 14 – Change Something

Day 15 – Start Something

Day 16 – Quit Something

Day 17 – Accept Something

Day 18 – Forget Something

Day 19 – Remember Something

Day 20 – Redefine Something

Day 21 – Learn Something

Day 22 – Give Something

Day 23 – Notice Something

Day 24 – Solve Something

Day 25 – Pretend Something

Day 26 – Believe Something

Day 27 – Undo Something

Day 28 – Redo Something

Day 29 – Discover Something

Day 30 – Suggest Something

Day 31 – Resist Something

Day 32 – Name Something

Day 33 – Refuse Something

Day 34 – Decide Something

Day 35 – Endorse Something

Day 36 – Deny Something

Day 37 – Send Something

Day 38 – Approve of Something/Someone

Day 39 – Improve Something

Day 40 – Share Something

Day 41 – Open Something

Day 42 – Close Something

Day 43 – Risk Something

Day 44 – Ask Someone

Day 45 – Trust Someone

Day 46 – Study Something

Day 47 – Surprise Someone

Day 48 – Forgive Someone

Day 49 – Inspire Someone

Day 50 – Understand Something

Day 51 – Clean Something

Day 52 – Liberate Someone

Day 53 – Love Someone

Day 54 – Appreciate Someone

Day 55 – Entertain Someone

Day 56 – Finish Something

Day 57 – Describe Something

Day 58 – Help Someone

Day 59 – Thank Someone

Day 60 – Shock Someone

Day 61 – Debate Something

Day 62 – Stretch Yourself

Day 63 – Treat Yourself

Day 64 – Rescue Something

Day 65 – Create Something

I'm really tempted to look at that list with a view to improving it. I jotted it down more than four years ago in a burst of inspiration and in about half an hour. What if … no, that's absurd.

Oh, go on, then, I'll say it anyway. What if I was meant to make that list and devise the 65 Days experiment in order that, several years later, I could find it again and use it to solve the happiness mystery? Could it be that this is precisely what Fate intended?

If I look at the list again now, I'm bound to want to make some substitutions. And … I don't think I'm going to give myself permission to do that. My list feels like an important historical artefact. I feel as if I need to obey it to the letter.

Wait – obey it? Does that mean that I'm going to do the experiment? I can't. I just can't, not on top of everything else I have to do.

A voice in my head says, *Yes, you can, and you should. You must.* (I strongly suspect this voice of causing all my problems. We may have a culprit, folks.)

In this instance, could the voice be right? Having looked again at the list, it seems to me that many of the items would not take too much time to achieve.

Sod it: I'm in. Let's go.

10

Practising the 65 Days

Look, if my future crime novel's heroine would let anyone bend the rules it would surely be me, her creator. Exactly. I agree. And so, while I haven't done 65 days yet, I have properly completed some of the tasks, on a one-item-per-day basis; and on one day I planned what I would do on some, though not all, of the remaining special-purpose days.

The results have been startling. This has made me happier than any other part of my investigation. I feel so much better, and am certainly going to carry on with the 65 Days – not because I think it will help me to solve the mystery of happiness, but simply because it's fun. It turns out that a concrete, thought-provoking list of Actual Stuff To Do is so much more enjoyable and mood-enhancing than endless frustrated musings about what happiness might or might not be. It occurs to me that the 65 Days could be my equivalent of Gretchen Rubin's Happiness Project. (Have I just plagiarised the work of my fictional heroine? Probably. She says she's fine with it, though.)

Here is where I'm up to, anyway (and I swapped the order around a bit too):

Day 1 – Promise Something

I promise that, from now on, in making all future plans, I will not overcommit myself.

Day 2 – Admit Something

I have admitted to myself that for years I have been acting in a way that is not in my long-term best interests: driving myself too hard and risking my physical and emotional health.

Day 3 – Invent Something

I invented two things that don't exist but, in my opinion, should:

1. Nice, inspiring health warnings that aren't so

much warnings (which are always depressing) as titbits of health inspiration. So, for example, on a packet of cigarettes, instead of photos of blackened limb stumps after amputation or hideous tumours on the insides of mouths, you could have a picture of a pink, healthy lung with the caption, 'You too can have shell-pink lungs if you give up smoking!' Frankly, I cannot believe that those in charge of health policy haven't thought of this already. It's hardly New Age or controversial to say that our mental health affects our physical health. Yes, smoking might cause cancer, but put it this way: are distressing images of horrendous disfigurement likely to create a state of mind that boosts anyone's immune system? Show smokers something lovely to aim for, not a terrifying vision of their bleakest possible future.

2. Confusion Laws. Some things are too wrong to be made legally permissible, and at the same time understandable enough that you'd never want to send anyone to prison for doing them. For this specific category of understandable offence, there ought to be something called a Confusion Law: it is absolutely wrong, and a crime in every official sense, but no one is ever punished for doing it.

Day 4 – Test Something

When I have some free time, I'm going to start testing perfumes regularly. I used to do this a lot when I lived in Manchester and I want to start doing it again. Perfume is one of my favourite things in the world.

Day 5 – Buy Something

I went to the Etsy website to search for something beautiful to buy. After rejecting lots of things because I knew I could live without them, I bought an absolutely beautiful and completely unnecessary bone china jug with a blue octopus painted on it. It was the first thing I saw that was irresistible, and is now sitting on the mantelpiece in the TV room. My evenings are enhanced by seeing it there every day.

Day 6 – Invite Someone

This one required me to overcome some of my British reserve. I'm going to Fort Collins, Colorado, early next May to give a keynote speech at a mystery writers' conference. One of my favourite life-coach podcasters, Tiffany Han, lives in Fort Collins. I emailed her and said, 'I'm a complete stranger who loves your podcast – I'd love to take you out for lunch or dinner when I'm in Fort Collins and chat about coaching and self-help.'

Day 7 – Write to Someone

I will write to my best friend from school, whom I haven't seen for years.

Day 8 – Remove Something

I finally threw away the manky old bedspread that Brewster, my dog, had chewed to pieces. Doing it still felt like too much effort, but once the thing was out of my house, I felt so much better.

Day 9 – Plan Something

I planned some of the other 65 Days activities that I'm going to do on future 'special purpose' days.

Day 10 – Cancel Something

I loved this one, as you can imagine. I cancelled three things that were in my diary that I had agreed to because it had seemed easier at the time. Each cancellation felt like a weight being lifted off my heart.

Day 11 – Start Something

I'm going to spring-clean my house, room by room, and throw away absolutely everything I don't want or need.

Day 12 – Quit something

I decided to cut sugar, flour and alcohol out of my diet (with the exception of occasional treats like dim sum, which I could never give up altogether). Why? Because Brooke recommends it, and I'm still feeling disciple-ish towards her, and I needed to lose weight, which I am doing with great success. All my rings are falling off my fingers. (I must admit, this is also partly because I have no time to eat any more.)

Day 13 – Accept Something

I am going to work on accepting that schools do not always treat children kindly or fairly (I feel as if this might take me more than a day to accomplish, and that's not allowed according to the terms of the 65 Days. I'll have to get up at 4 a.m. to stand even a tiny chance of succeeding.)

Day 14 – Redefine Something

I have redefined what the words 'a productive day' mean to me. I used to regard a day as productive only if I did absolutely everything on my to-do list for that day. From now on, a productive day is any day on which I accomplish one good and important thing.

Day 15 – Give Something

I'm going to give all the books and bound proofs in the house that I no longer want to St Botolph's Church in Cambridge, where my husband is a member of the choir.

Day 16 – Notice something

I'm going to notice that whenever I focus only on my own behaviour/thinking, and don't try to control the behaviour of other people, I feel much more at peace, in a deep and stoical Marcus Aurelius-ish way.

Day 17 – Name Something

I have named lots of things. I needed a name for the chat forum part of my Dream Author coaching programme, and I have decided to call it the Talking Point. I've also named two of my future dogs: Bernie Leadoff and Furbert Lemons. These are the dogs I'm going to get when I work less hard and can bribe my husband with promises to do more dog-related chores instead of leaving them all to him. Some people think Bernie Leadoff is not a good name for a dog you love because it sounds like Bernie Madoff, but: a) that's the joke – that very thing; b) the similarity of name in no way implies similarity of moral character; and c) a dachshund or wire fox terrier is highly unlikely to mastermind a fraudulent Ponzi scheme.

Day 18 – Forgive Someone

I will try to forgive the people I love who voted for something I regard as evil in recent elections. (This will be very hard. I expect to encounter a lot of 'forgiveness resistance', and I will have to get up even earlier for this one than for Day 13's task.)

Day 19 – Finish Something

I finished an article I'd promised to write for a collection of essays by crime writers about the craft and practice of crime writing. I had agreed reluctantly to do it, and had secretly planned to let the deadline pass, and then pretend to have accidentally missed it. I decided instead to fulfil the commitment I'd made. So I started it, finished it and emailed it in.

Day 20 – Rescue Something

I was asked to write a golden age murder mystery story for a magazine, and once again was induced by my foolish Bertrand-Russell-style zest to say yes. I rescued an idea that I'd used years earlier in an immature and thankfully unpublished short story, and used the very same mystery-and-solution combination as the basis for a far better story.

Is the 65 Days, then, my answer to the mystery of happiness? Is it all I need? If it's an experiment rather than an answer, how can it be the answer?

There's something I need to do before I can declare this case closed.

11

Final Session with a Life Coach

Her name is Diana, and I'm talking to her on Skype. She's British, not American. I decided it was time to stop putting American life coaches on a pedestal and try one closer to home instead. I start our session by explaining why.

Me: I think I'm addicted to escaping. In all areas of my life. American life coaches feel so far away from my real life, and I have an innate bias that keeps whispering, 'The further away from your reality, the better'. The fact that you're English and I could get in my car if I wanted to and drive to where you are in two hours makes this feel so much more as if it's actually happening, and less

like I'm the screwed-up heroine of a Hollywood
movie – not that they'd ever let someone who
wears a shrunk-in-the-wash pink cashmere cardy
over a blue Adidas T-shirt star in a Hollywood
movie. Sorry about my appearance, by the way.
I have no idea where all my proper clothes are.
Soon as I finish the book I'm writing about
happiness, I'm buying some new clothes.

Her: Tell me about your happiness book.

Me: It's kind of interesting. I *really* wanted to
write it at first, then when I started, I found I
wasn't enjoying it at all. I'd made life too difficult
for myself by pitching it as a mystery. The
publishers loved that idea, because I'm a crime
writer so it seemed apt, but … I'm a traditional
crime writer. I believe mysteries need to have
proper solutions. And … what if the mystery of
happiness can't be solved decisively?

Her: I don't think it can.

Me: Of course it can! Thank you, you've just
strengthened my resolve. I'm very contrary.
I sometimes think contrariness is my main
characteristic.

Her: How do you know the mystery of happiness can be solved?

Me: It has to be if I'm not willing to consider any other possibility, which I'm not. I know there's a solution to be had, and I know I'm not there yet, and that's fine *because* … I can kind of feel myself getting closer. The 65 Days was a step in the right direction but it wasn't it: the one true answer.

Her: What's the 65 Days?

Me: It doesn't matter. It'd take way too long to explain. I don't want to waste any of this session. I decided in advance: this is my last session with a life coach – at least until the mystery's solved. I've been procrastinating by talking to life coaches, and I'm not going to solve the mystery that way.

Her: Then why did you book this session at all?

Me: I have no idea! I just … I wanted to. I like life coaching. I've had therapy but I prefer coaching. But I've got an addictive personality, and I could so easily spend all day every day getting coached and then I'd get no work done. And now I have an added incentive to finish all my work – because I've resolved to do *hardly any* work for the rest of my life, as soon as I've done all the work I've already agreed to do. Apart from running my coaching programme – I'll still do that, but that feels more like an amazing hobby than work. Though I guess that's easy to say before I've actually started it.

Her: More escapism?

Me: I mean … in my defence, can I just say that I do actually get a hell of a lot done?

Her: Does that matter? Wouldn't you be just as valuable as a person if you got nothing done?

Me: Yes. Obviously. Brewster, my dog, does nothing all day and he's the most valuable person in the world. I'm much stricter on myself, though. I think most people are – we reserve our harshest criticisms for ourselves. It's funny …

Her: What is?

Me: I've got a friend who's a psychotherapist, and I was talking to her recently about my reluctance to tell anyone, ever, if they've upset or annoyed me. We were discussing how this tendency of mine is very likely to be a result of feeling mildly to moderately tyrannised when I was younger ... and then, later, I thought of something really weird. For the last six years, I haven't felt *at all* tyrannised by other human beings. Like, there's no one on the planet from whom I fear oppression or bullying ... and for the exact same length of time that that has been true, it has *also* been true that I've felt that my work is a kind of oppressive tyrant stalker figure. Those were the exact words I used the first time I spoke to a life coach about it.

Her: That is interesting.

Me: Yeah. Maybe – because the brain likes to stick to familiar habits and fears change, doesn't it? – maybe I don't feel comfortable unless there's an oppressive tyrant in my life, and so, when I ran out of human contenders for the position, I made my work 'It'.

Her: You do sound as if you've been talking to a psychotherapist!

Me: Hey, don't diss therapy. I love therapy *and* coaching.

Her: I'm more interested in what you're going to do in the future than what's happened in the past.

Me: I've told you: hardly any work, as soon as possible. No more deadlines. That's in the long term—

Her: So, not that soon, then!

Me: In the short term, I'm going to … You know what I'm going to do, actually? I'm going to set a denouement date.

Her: A what?

I explain to Diana that part of my crime-writing work involves writing new Poirot novels, and that Poirot, at the end of the adventures in which he stars, has a penchant for gathering the suspects together in the drawing room (or sometimes a different room) and presenting them with his brilliantly deduced solution to the mystery.

Her: And you're going to do that with your happiness mystery?

Me: Yes. That's what Poirot did in the third novel I wrote about him, *The Mystery of Three Quarters*. He was growing impatient with his inability to solve the mystery, so he invited all the suspects to Combingham Hall on a particular date at a particular time – then he knew he had no choice but to solve the mystery by that time.

Her: So you're going to set yourself a deadline, effectively?

Me: Yes!

Her: When you talked about deadlines before in relation to your writing, you sounded resentful about them.

Me: Well, it's obviously different if the deadline is mine rather than someone else's. I'm a questioner, not an upholder or an obliger. Have you read *The Four Tendencies* by Gretchen Rubin?

Her: No.

Me: Have you heard of Brooke Castillo?

Her: No.

Bloody hell. Should I slam my laptop lid shut and pretend we got cut off? Has Diana even read Agatha Christie? I daren't ask.

Me: Poirot set himself a deadline to sharpen his mind, and that's what I'm going to do too. The more people I invite to my denouement scene, the more embarrassing it'll be if I fail to come up with a solution in time. Do you mind if I ask you … what do you think happiness is? Do you feel as if you personally have solved the mystery of happiness? And is it too broad an idea? Like, I could easily advise someone on how to be happy in relation to parenting – there's a brilliant book by Shefali Tsabary called *The Conscious Parent* – and in relation to writing, I know exactly how to be happy, which is why I'm creating my Dream Author programme—

Her: Really? What are you going to tell the people who join the programme about how to be happy as a writer?

Me: The first and most important thing I'm going to tell them is … Oh. My. God.

Her: What?

Me: Diana! I'm so glad I didn't slam my laptop shut!

Her: I don't understand.

Me: You've done it! You've done what I've consistently failed to do. God, I've been so stupid! *How* did I not see it? This is what happens just before a denouement, by the way. Always. Damn! Now I don't need the threat of a well-attended Denouement Day to sharpen my mind because I've solved the mystery – thanks to you. And, fuck it, in the large majority of Poirot novels, he only gathers people for the denouement once he knows all the answers. I'm going to do it anyway.

Her: Do what?

Me: Denouement Day!

12

Denouement Day

We are gathered in the drawing room. Well, sort of. It probably was once called by that name, but since we've owned this house it's been known as the TV room. I have an audience of four for my denouement scene, and one of them is my dog, Brewster. The other three are my husband, Dan, and my two teenage children, Phoebe (17) and Guy (15).

It's now or never. So it's now.

I have purposefully chosen the thought, 'I have my ideal audience here today and it couldn't be more perfect'. I am managing to believe this thought even though, where fifteen-year-old boys are concerned, there's a thin line between eagerly awaiting the denouement of a suspenseful mystery about the nature of happiness and a grudging willingness to remain in the room in exchange for new sportswear.

My husband, like me, is a questioner-tipping-to-rebel. Once while we were watching the denouement scene of a David Suchet Poirot episode, he said irritably, 'Why do they all just sit there and let Poirot accuse them of stuff? I'd get up and walk out.'

He looks ready to challenge me, though he has no idea what I'm about to say. My daughter is interested but doing her best to pretend not to be. Brewster looks as if he can't understand what all the fuss is about, since the correct answer is obvious: happiness is steak, and/or cheese, followed by an endless game of 'Throwy' with his orange rubber ball.

'Okay,' I begin. 'So, you know I've been trying to solve the mystery of happiness?'

'No,' says Guy. 'Mum, how long's this gonna take? I wanna go to Lily's.'

'Vaguely,' says Phoebe.

'I thought you were writing a book about it, not solving a mystery,' says Dan.

'The book is about the solving of the mystery. Anyway, I've been doing all this research and reading and making longlists and shortlists, and listening and talking to life coaches—'

'Are you gonna start banging on about Brooke Castillo again?' Phoebe narrows her eyes.

'Yes! Thanks for reminding me. I've worked out how to resolve my one area of disagreement with Brooke, and it turns out that we don't disagree at all. We just use different terminology. She sent out an email recently – I'm on her mailing list, three times over, actually – in which she described how she decided not to employ a particular florist. This woman came to her house, and Brooke overheard her being rude to a member of her staff and so decided not to employ her, and in the email she wrote something like, "I wasn't going to give her my business because she'd shown me who she really was." When I read that, I realised that Brooke's way and my way, or what I think is probably the ideal way of relating to other people, from a happiness point of view, are not as different as I imagined they were. They might not even be different at all!'

'What are you on about?' says Guy.

'Do you actually want to know?' Phoebe snaps at him. He is polite enough to limit his response to a half-shrug.

'Never mind,' I press on. 'The point is, if Brooke allows herself to decide that someone is rude and that she doesn't want to employ them, that means she thinks it's okay both to acknowledge grudge-worthy behaviour, even if she would never call it that, *and* to change her thoughts and actions in relation to a purveyor of grudge-worthy behaviour. I reckon that when she talks about unconditional love, she means a sort of general well-wishing spirit towards all humans and an awareness that we're all fallible and all doing our best – which, again, I totally agree with. She doesn't mean what *I* mean by love.'

'So you totally agree with Brooke,' says Dan. 'Is that the answer, then? Agreeing with Brooke?'

'No. It's just something I'm pleased about, because I love Brooke.'

'But it's not the solution to the mystery of happiness?' asks Phoebe.

'No.'

'Then what is? I'm not being funny, but I've got a philosophy essay to write by tomorrow morning.'

'I'm getting there. In my last session with a life coach, Diana, I told her I thought it would be easier to define what constituted happiness in relation to specific things. I'd told her about Dream Author and I said that I knew exactly what happiness meant for writers, and she said, "What are you going to tell the people who join your programme about how to be happy as a writer?", and as she said it, everything clicked into place!'

'What do you mean?' Dan asks.

'I've got a notebook full of Dream Author content and—'

'You have?' he cuts in. 'I thought you weren't starting it till September.'

'I've been making notes since last November,' I tell him. 'It's what I do when I'm supposed to be working and can't face it. One of the exercises I've created for

Dream Author – one of my very favourites, because it kind of contains the essence of the whole programme and the main lesson I want to teach anyone who joins – is called "The Best Result". Shall I read it to you?'

'If you must.'

'Go on.'

'How long's this going to last? Oh my God.'

'Ssh, Guy. Okay, the question is "What is the best result that any writer can get?" Then underneath that I've written, "I'm not going to explain any further at this stage. I'm very interested to see what you come up with. Try to write an answer that would be equally true for any writer, no matter what their genre is or where they're at in their writing journey." When Diana the life coach asked me what happiness means for writers specifically, my 'Best Result' exercise popped into my mind and I realised that the answer to that question was the solution to the mystery of happiness!'

'How?' says Phoebe. 'Explain.'

'The Dream Author exercise answer is this: "The best result for any writer is always to have a Dream-Goal that they are passionate about, totally committed to, and taking active steps towards achieving, and that they believe 100 per cent that they can and will achieve."'

'What?' Guy frowns. 'Isn't the best result getting as rich as J. K. Rowling?'

'Nope. Because you can be stinking rich and incredibly miserable. You can be a world-famous multi-million seller and be bored and lonely. Or oppressed by deadlines. Whereas if you're committed to a goal that you're happily working towards and believing you're going to get there—'

'So that's the answer: working towards a goal?' Phoebe sounds disappointed.

'No. The solution to the happiness puzzle isn't exactly the same, but it's so similar that thinking about the Dream Author 'Best Results' answer made me realise exactly what the solution to the mystery of happiness is. Want to hear it?'

'Yeah.'

'Get on with it.'

'Mum, this is torture. I wanna go and see Lily.'

I freeze. I don't want to tell them, in case saying it out loud ruins the perfection of it. It really is perfect. Nothing will convince me that it isn't.

'Happiness is actively and passionately working to solve the mystery of happiness, while totally believing that there *is* a solution and that you're going to find it. And that means … it means I could have been perfectly happy all this time, except I wasn't 100 per cent convinced I would be able to definitively solve the mystery! But now I am, because I have!'

Everyone stares at me, apart from Brewster who fell asleep a few minutes ago.

'I'm right,' I announce after a short silence. That's why the 65 Days felt so much like moving in the right direction – it required more than simply contemplating and comparing theories. It involved taking active steps to solve the mystery of happiness, while believing that I could and would. (The believing part is vital. If you don't believe you're going to get there, you won't be able to feel amazing en route.) And there's no element of bad-crime-novel anti-climactic resolution to the 65 Days, because it's a *search* rather than an answer, and as I said in the introduction to this book, definite answers shut down possibilities, while an unsolved puzzle ignites our imagination.

That's why my solution to the mystery of happiness is so neat and satisfying: the solution is the continuing search for the solution. You could say that it's trying to have its cake and eat it, but that would be churlish. I prefer to think that it offers the joy of ongoing possibility in combination with the certainty of resolution, and with neither one detracting from the other.

I love it.

I am filled with Poirovian certainty. I *know* my answer is the correct one. No one – not Aristotle, not Bertrand Russell and not even Brooke Castillo – has come up with anything so short, elegant and right.

And yet …

13

The Twist at the End

Today is Day 66. I'm at one of the most stunning hotels I've ever stayed in: the five-star Shangri-La in London, in the Shard building. It has staggering views of this beautiful city that I am in so often but never really look at because I'm always marching with my head down, praying I won't bump into anyone I know because even a three-minute chat would make me late for seventeen meetings.

That's right: I'm happy to report that my day-to-day life has not yet changed in any way. It's still bonkers and unsustainable, and I'm still very happy with it – far happier than is good for me. My stair carpets, for example, are so severely in need of a hoovering that I can barely see what colour they are any more, and I don't much care. One day I'll let my cleaner come and sort it out, or my husband will notice and do it;

that's good enough for me.

(In case you're wondering, the emergency carpet situation has arisen because I've cancelled my cleaner three times in a row. I've got some big deadlines looming, not to mention my son's mock GCSEs – and please don't think that this is a matter only for his attention and not mine; gone are those days, as any parent of a contemporary teenager will confirm – and the thought of having someone in my house that I have to exchange even three words with that aren't swearwords is something I can't face at the moment. I know some people don't chat to their cleaners, but it's impossible for me to allow someone in my house to go un-chatted to – therefore, it's scruffy dog-hair-covered carpets for the win! That's my new thought and it's working beautifully.)

The carpet situation at home makes me appreciate the immaculate luxury of the Shangri-La even more. This hotel has the highest swimming pool in western Europe, which I cannot wait to swim in. At the moment I'm sitting on a lounger beside it, with my laptop balanced on a folded bathrobe on my knees. This purpose of this weekend trip is to celebrate my daughter's seventeenth birthday. It's also my present to myself for solving the mystery of happiness. As if that weren't enough, it is Day 66 of the experiment that I'm still pursuing, and still calling the 65 Days, even though, as you can see, I'm invoking Inventor's

Privilege and adding a 66th. Why? Because this book will be published in 2020, which is a leap year. We get an extra day, so it might as well be a 'special purpose' day rather than an ordinary one.

So. Day 66: Twist Something. Or Add a Twist to Something, maybe. That sounds better. Because although I've solved the mystery of happiness, I can now reveal that (as so often in mystery stories) there's a further twist.

Here's the problem: I have found a logical contradiction in my solution to the mystery of happiness. I know, dear sidekick – you were being tactful and not mentioning it, but I'm afraid we'd better face it head-on.

If the solution to the mystery of happiness is actively and passionately working to solve the mystery of happiness, that suggests that one must believe one hasn't already solved it. Because if it's already solved, why would you bother putting in the effort? That means I have to choose: either I can pursue the mystery of happiness, full of zestful confidence that I can and will solve it, or else I can believe I've already solved it, in which case there's nothing to pursue. Anything else would be an illogical continuity error.

I prefer the pursuit and the mystery, so that's what I'm choosing. Which means I need to believe I haven't solved anything, and that's not so hard to do. All thoughts and beliefs are optional, after all. And, let's face it, what are the chances that a crime writer with frizzy hair and unhoovered carpets could solve such a profound mystery so quickly and easily?

So, on with the next phase of the investigation, which will take place in a five-star hotel's swimming pool. There's no time to lose! Let's solve this thing!

Acknowledgements

I would like to thank my wonderful agent Peter Straus and his team at Rogers, Coleridge & White; everybody at Profile Books and the Wellcome Trust; Dan, Phoebe, Guy and Brewster; Susanne Hillen; Helen Acton; Naomi Alderman; and all the therapists and life coaches who have helped me to improve my life significantly over the years, especially Brooke Castillo.

Wellcome collection is the free visitor destination for the incurably curious. It explores the connections between medicine, life and art in the past, present and future. Wellcome Collection is part of the Wellcome Trust, a global charitable foundation dedicated to improving health by supporting bright minds in science, the humanities and social sciences, and public engagement.